OSCAR WILDE'S CRUCIFIX

CRUCIFIX

A BIOGRAPHICAL EXPERIMENT

MAARTEN ASSCHER

FOUR WINDS
PRESS

OSCAR WILDE'S CRUCIFIX
A Biographical Experiment

The chapters set in roman type are strictly based on historical fact. In the chapters printed in italics the author has allowed his imagination to supply the story with additional insights.

Four Winds Press
San Francisco, CA

Print ISBN. 978-1-940423-21-0
Ebook ISBN. 978-1-94023-22-7

Cover and interior design by Domini Dragoone

9 8 7 6 5 4 3 2 1

Distributed in the US by Publishers Group West
Distributed in the UK by Ingram
Distributed in The Netherlands and Belgium by De Bezige Bij

IN MEMORY OF JBWP

CONTENTS

PREFACE

Biography is both the most ambitious
and the most basic of literary genres.

Nothing is so unpredictable as the past.

In the retelling of one individual human life
all literary forms and forces converge.

Chance only convinces in real life. In books
and in films, what is presented as accidental,
invariably impresses one as improbable.

Details are nearly always more important than details,
just as essentials are very often less than essential.

Every curiosity is based on a degree of exaggeration.

The media seem to think that of all human talents,
youth is the most enviable, and the annoying thing
is that they are completely right.

All that is really interesting, is complicated,
but not all that is complicated is also interesting.

>Believable facts and lifelike characters
>are no guarantee for an accomplished story;
>on the contrary, these are among the obstacles
>that the author must surmount.

Artists and writers should only make work for which they
feel uniquely suited. All the rest they should leave to others.

>To tell 'the whole truth and nothing but the truth'
>is impossible.

The fleeting moment and the individual
human being are the small change left on the table,
once the historians have left to write their books.

>The more you make up in a book,
>the more personal it will become.

If you tell the same story in other words,
you tell a different story.

>Classifying books in genres is for librarians
>and shopkeepers; writers and readers should
>prowl around as freely as possible and not let
>themselves be kept on a leash.

A lie is the more plausible,
if it contains a kernel of truth.

Imagination is far more unreliable than memory.

A thought not put into words,
is not yet a thought.

Everything a book strives for in terms of depth,
must be accomplished on the surface of the language.

If one makes historical facts into a narrative,
one is fictionalising, even if the resulting book
is called a biography.

The truth, if it exists, can only be revealed by
the imagination.

Every biography,
like every life itself,
is an experiment.

1

THE END

*Reginald Turner looks at the face that until recently
was so familiar to him, but which now—day after
day, hour after hour—is losing more and more of its
features. Gradually, the colour is disappearing from
the cheeks and neck, and perhaps it is only thanks to
the dim afternoon light in the room that the worsen-
ing condition of the patient is not more clearly visible.
Against the right temple, there is a bag of ice on the
pillow to ease the pain.*

*The calm suggested by the sleeping breath is
not just deceptive, Reginald fears, but also ominous.
Behind the closed eyelids a storm probably rages. And
the pain? Since the embassy doctor has forbidden
the administration of more opium, a fake injection is
occasionally given. Would that still have an effect, or
has his consciousness already sunk so deep that pain
can no longer reach him?*

*With some trepidation, Reggie thinks about the
ear surgery that was performed. Even though he did
not attend the operation himself, the detailed account*

*he received gave him the feeling not just of having been
present, but even of having undergone the surgery
himself. The essence of pain is so personal that it cannot be felt by someone else, but if you cannot stand
pain, something Reggie admitted to himself long ago
as a boy, it is almost impossible to bear the suffering
of another.*

*A month and a half has passed since that opera-
tion, and the patient now lies motionless on his back,
supported by extra pillows. Listening to the regular
breathing, you might think he is still doing rather
well, but involuntarily Reggie imagines the incoherent
thoughts and fears that flutter through his friend's
brain like bats in the dark: nights in a clammy cell,
insults on the street, deep pain in his head. Being
dead is peace, but dying is a war against superhuman
forces. The oppressive silence in the room feels thick
and warm, and the rushing, sometimes slightly rasp-
ing breathing from the bed mixes with the whoosh of
the gas stove.*

*Except for a narrow strip of light, the curtains have
been drawn. Sometimes a silhouette flashes by on the
pavement. On this sombre November afternoon it seems
as if it is already evening, and in the semi-darkness
the flowered wallpaper has been reduced to a brown-
ish grey. Occasionally, the hotel room door is quietly
opened. Mostly it is the hotel owner Dupoirier who
comes to take a look at how his locataire is doing, or
the embassy doctor, for a brief check-up. This morning,
the doctor was decidedly pessimistic, just like yesterday.
There is little change and certainly no improvement, he*

intimated. The doctor has strange ways of checking the condition of his patient. For example, he asked the sick man yesterday—or was it the day before?—to whistle, and nodded in the affirmative when he could not. What is that supposed to mean?

The patient hardly reacts to movements in the room anymore. Reggie himself feels sluggish, due to lack of sleep and because of the stuffiness in the room, yet he wants to take in every detail, every little change. After all, this deathbed will also be a decisive scene in his own life, and what he experiences here deserves the greatest possible attention. In clearer moments, Reggie is very aware of a special responsibility, now that he is the only one of so many friends who keeps watch in this room.

They first met just seven years ago, at one of those unforgettable dinners at the Monico, but it seems so much longer. So far, there has been no one in his life whom he has befriended so intimately in such a short time, despite—or perhaps because of—the disastrous interruption of two full years. Their age difference of fifteen years played no noticeable role. Did the unstoppable energy and youthful dynamism of the now-dying poet redeem me of being an old fogey, Reggie wonders, or did their friendly gatherings and dinners have something ageless about them anyway? In any case, there are not many people who have expe-rienced such highs and lows in quick succession.

The first night of A Woman of No Importance *was followed by a series of great theatrical triumphs, cut short by the fatal trials and the arrest in that London hotel room. That terrible wait for the inevitable arrival of the police. The minutes ticking away, reducing the possibility of a flight, if that had ever been the intention. Robbie and he had looked at each other a few times, with the unspoken thought of running off and taking their friend against his will, if necessary, but slowly they had become convinced of the futility of such an attempt. In the end, the three of them had sat paralysed, waiting for the inevitable. Now, Reggie is once again in a hotel room, waiting for another irreversible mischief to befall his friend. And this time, the impending doom is even larger; larger than the human brain can grasp.*

    Until a few days ago, there was a male nurse who understood the art of being present almost imperceptibly and who nevertheless did everything that needed to be done: taking care of the surgical wound, changing the bandages, applying mustard plasters. After working several days and nights in a row, the young man had to give up due to fatigue. Maurice Gilbert also came by a few times, but he could not do much, except promise that he would come again soon. Now it is the loyal Reggie Turner who holds the hand of his dying friend for a while. That feels good, even if the patient will hardly notice, because it suggests that he means something, that he offers some kind of support. With his other hand, Reggie pulls out his watch. Did he hear a carriage halt in front of the hotel? He would like to get up and look out the window.

    Reggie spent the night at the hotel, in a room upstairs, but this morning at about five o'clock he was

*already back at the bedside, as was the embassy doctor
who had also spent the night here. At half-past eleven
Robbie finally arrived, having immediately returned
by train from Menton. Reggie had kept him informed
by letter over the past few days, but in the end a brief
message by telegram had sufficed to indicate the seriousness of the situation. Dupoirier had also stressed
the urgency of Monsieur Ross's return.*

*They hugged each other emotionally, even though
they had seen and spoken to each other at length just
two weeks ago. In that short period the situation had
considerably worsened, and after consulting with the
doctor and with the hotel owner about things that
were needed urgently, Robbie had gone into town to
make several arrangements.*

*Dupoirier regularly comes to see how his guest is
doing. These last few weeks the patron has been the
epitome of caring hospitality, providing the patient
with fresh water and ice and even administering
injections himself, while also attending to friends
and visitors and to the two doctors by bringing coffee,
tea and bread and ordering hot meals. The ear surgery performed in the hotel must have caused much
consternation, yet Reggie had not heard a single com-
plaint from the loyal Dupoirier. The patron had even
told him with a certain pride that he had been busy for
hours that day with hot water and cloths, with coffee
for both the doctors and the nurse and with brandy for
the patient. The sweet chloroform smell had lingered
for a long time, giving the room and the corridors the
atmosphere of a hospital rather than a hotel. Of course,*

*there had been no question of opening a window, not
then and not even now, unfortunately, if only ajar.*

*'Comment ça va?' asks Dupoirier, closing the door
gently behind him. As if it were the patient trying
to give an answer, a soft moan sounds from the
bed, followed by a momentary deep hum, in which
some fragments of English and French words can be
discerned. Reggie gently wiggles his head and purses his
lips, to signify that the situation has not changed much.
The hotelier, as always with a white cloth over his left
shoulder, silently picks up an empty plate and two
coffee cups from the small table and leaves the room.*

*Yesterday, the patient suddenly tried to get out of
bed. He wanted to drink and half got up, which apparently gave him the idea to get out of bed. He would
never have been able to stand on his own two feet and
Reggie had a lot of trouble getting him back into the
pillows with all kinds of soothing words. It was quite
a relief once he lay still on his back again. So close to
him, Reggie had felt the warmth of the feverish and
sweaty forehead.*

*Now he looks for the umpteenth time at the closed
eyelids, at this precious face that has lost so much of
its fullness in such a short time. Only two or three
weeks ago, when the ear surgery appeared to have
succeeded and at least some recovery was evident, the
three of them had lunch at a nearby restaurant and
the conversation had seemed as usual. As so often,
they had been drinking champagne unconcernedly in
the middle of the day, while Robbie and Reggie knew
full well that this daily consumption of alcohol was*

both an expensive and an unwise indulgence for their sick friend. But both these arguments had never made much of an impression on him, so they had refrained from making a point of it.

The half-long hair lies in wisps over the large forehead. Next to the bag of ice, some of the hair has been shaved away to make room for two leeches, with a view to relieving the pressure on the brain. Reggie looks at the leeches and shudders. To him the whole idea of bloodsucking is abhorrent, as if vampires are attacking his dear friend's head.

Reggie remembers how his friend was always trying to choose just the right hairstyle for a certain stage in his life and in his artistic development. Once, short and somewhat curled to rule over his admirers like a Roman emperor; later, long and undulating, to illustrate his aesthetic ideals to the public. Holloway's prison barber for one had not cared about such fashionable preferences. In his mind's eye, Reggie still sees him standing on the forward deck of the ferry, with that short hair, on arrival in Dieppe, when Robbie and he had stayed up all night to welcome the exile to the Normandy harbour. In the still-foggy early morning light they had run towards the boat over the harbour head, waving, cheering.

Reggie must have fallen asleep for a while because he is startled when around four o'clock Robbie enters the hotel room in a hurry, followed by a priest who introduces himself with a handshake as Father Cuthbert Dunne, then takes off his coat and puts it over one of the chairs. Father Dunne is probably no older than thirty, but from the careful way in which he bends over the bed and gently rouses the dying man, who lifts his hand in greeting, it is clear that he has the necessary experience. From his bag, he begins to pull out various attributes.

As a non-Catholic, Reggie gently rises and leaves the room so as not to hinder the men in their delicate pursuits. He suddenly feels how incredibly tired he actually is. On the landing he finds Dupoirier, who stands at the door in respectful anticipation. Together they remain silent, while rumbling and mumbling sounds can be heard from the room. Reggie cannot understand the words that are being spoken, but he can see from the hotelier's moving lips that he knows exactly what is presently being said and done. Reggie feels very involved in everything; at the same time he knows that he is an outsider to the ritual that now takes place on the other side of the thin wall. What would it be like, he silently wonders, to exchange the inadequacy of reason for a surrender to faith at the very end of your life? Would that make death more acceptable? The beauty of rituals is alluring, Reggie can feel their attraction, but how to draw the right conclusions without taking a step into the void?

On the other side of the door, in room 13 of the Hôtel d'Alsace on the rue des Beaux-Arts, in the sixth arrondissement of Paris, Father Cuthbert Dunne of the Congregation of the Passionists pronounces the formulas of conditional baptism and of the Blessed Sacrament of the Sick and ascertains the consenting reactions—however weak and inarticulate—of the *dying Oscar Wilde. A day later, on the 30th of November, 1900, the forty-six-year-old writer will breathe his last at ten to two in the afternoon.*

On this, the penultimate day of his life, with the little consciousness left to him, he has his ultimate, more or less clear perception, when he opens his eyes and turns his gaze to the dangling little golden crucifix around the neck of the young priest, who administers the anointment to his forehead and thus receives him caringly into the arms of the Roman Catholic Church. Then the patient sinks into depths from which no return is possible.

2

IN LOVE

The passing of Oscar Wilde is one of the most moving death scenes in English literary history, alongside that of John Keats, Lord Byron and Virginia Woolf. In the hundreds of biographies that have been written about the Irish writer, this elongated moment is rightly one of the key episodes. The final scene shares this prominent place in every telling of his life's story, from his birth on the 16th of October, 1854, onwards, along with his academic triumphs as a student in Dublin and at Oxford; his year-long lecture tour of America; the first nights of his immensely successful plays in London; his meeting and love affair with Lord Alfred Douglas and the witch hunt by the latter's father, the Marquess of Queensberry; and of course the three fateful trials, culminating in a two-year prison sentence for *gross indecency*, that is, sex with other men.

When I say 'moving,' this should be taken in the most literal sense of the word. Descriptions of Wilde's last months, in which he is slowly but irrevocably nearing his end, always move me, no matter how many times I have read them in different versions. As far as I'm concerned, these passages evoke a wide range of emotions—sadness, pity, indignation and anger—while at the same time rekindling my admiration for Wilde's strength of spirit, his supreme sense of humour and his contempt for bourgeois society and its institutions that were intent on bringing him down. This emotional affinity with the life and fate of Oscar Wilde is not easy to interpret, but at the start of this biographical experiment it makes sense to say something about it, from which in any case it will be clear that this predilection goes back a long way.

The bookcase in my childhood home had once been a mirror frame. Bookshelves were mounted in the place where the mirror glass used to be, within a casing added to the rear. The symbolism of this transformation was, probably unintentionally, perfect. In fact, the mirror effect worked in two ways: the contents of the shelves reflected the taste of my parents, and I, as a child, found in that bookcase the necessary traits for my still immature personality. The bookcase was neither high nor wide, containing perhaps one hundred and fifty books, but precisely because of its modest size, for a child this collection had an accessible clarity, which in turn gave the individual books a greater specific gravity. Some books were disturbing from the start, such as the photo book *The Yellow Star* about the persecution of the Jews during the Second World War; others were incomprehensible *(The Phenomenon of Man* by P. Teilhard de Chardin) or inexhaustible (the *Encyclopaedia for Everyone*). Still others, such as James A. Michener's blockbuster novels or Piero Calamandrei's *Eulogy of Judges*, later proved ideal adversaries.

The book from this collection that has by far exercised the strongest attraction to this very day is Oscar Wilde's prison letter *De Profundis*. My reading as a teenager of that book was soon followed by the author's only novel, *The Picture of Dorian Gray*. The Irish writer was without a doubt the greatest miracle to emerge from this parental bookcase. As a reader I stepped, like Alice in Wonderland, into the literary world behind the mirror.

De profundis confronted me with the tragic life story of the author, and with his fate in successive English prisons. My first reading of this long and heartbreaking letter—a combination of indictment, creed, autobiography, admission of guilt, and declaration of love—perhaps sowed the seeds for the PhD thesis I would write half a century later, on imprisonment as a literary experience (*The Hour of Truth*, 2015), in which Oscar Wilde plays a significant role.

The Picture of Dorian Gray enchanted me with all the pleasures and vices, elegantly hinted at or suggestively disguised, that the main character Dorian Gray indulges in. These range from opium use and wanderings through nocturnal city slums to unspeakable missteps, the exact nature of which is deliberately never fully revealed. Whatever all those sins amount to, they leave no trace on the eternally youthful face of the novel's principal character. It is only in a portrait painted by his admirer Basil Hallward—hidden far away in the attic by Dorian—that his abject life shows its visible consequences.

In the novel, Dorian's mysterious misconduct is excused and in no small measure encouraged with brilliant epigrams by the somewhat older aesthete Lord Henry Wotton. What impressed me most from my first reading of the book was the suggestiveness, the seductiveness of the words with which all that is forbidden is presented to the main character and thereby also to the reader. All those vaguely transgressive words thus became themselves an evil force, as Wilde would experience personally during the cross-examination in his two criminal trials. Literary language can be as exciting as sexual stimulation. As a fourteen- or fifteen-year-old reader it was quite a revelation for me that with mere written words you can effectively stimulate someone's head, heart and even someone's body. It was an experience that certainly contributed to my lifelong conversion, not only to the work of this one writer, but to literature in general.

The Picture of Dorian Gray is a book that can change your life, as the young poet Lord Alfred Douglas himself would experience. It is no exaggeration to say that his infatuation with the seventeen-years older Oscar Wilde was first aroused by this novel. When the stunningly beautiful blonde Oxford student met his thirty-six-year-old idol in June 1891, he professed to have read *Dorian Gray* nine times already. Similarly, in the novel, Dorian Gray's head is turned by a book, a seductive book given by Lord Henry Wotton for him to read. Its title is not revealed, but from various references it is clear that the book is *À rebours* by Joris-Karl Huysmans, a sensual and exuberant French novel from 1884, sometimes referred to as 'the Bible of Decadentism'.

The fact that Wilde was convicted in London and thrown into prison in the very year of my dear English grandfather's birth, also made me consider him not as distant literary history, but as part of the living, still tangible memory. The house where my grandfather was born on the 5th of September, 1895, was no more than a few hundred meters away from the prison where Wilde was being held at the time, so I found out later.

The discovery of this writer not only marked the beginning of an immersion in his collected works and in his magnificent letters, but also led to an obsession for collecting books and studies about Wilde and his time. I must confess that I probably own more biographies about Oscar Wilde than is good for me. As he is such a complex and multifaceted figure, there is not one among the many hundreds of biographies about him that can be said to make all the others superfluous.

With many authors, artists or other public figures people talk about the appearance of the *definitive* biography; in the case of Oscar Wilde that claim is impossible. Every description of his life—whatever its literary or academic merits—adds aspects, interpretations and sometimes interesting facts, and to me any new biography of this writer is already attractive for the simple reason that this fascinating life story is told in a different way. Reading yet another Wilde-biography often feels like talking to someone about a mutual friend, so that the preciousness of the subject may compensate for any perceived shortcomings in the narrative.

The susceptibility of Wilde's life to successive generations of biographers has partly to do with the various identities that he encompassed: Wilde as a lifelong Catholic convert-to-be, as a brilliant classicist, as a broadly oriented literary journalist, as an art critic and magazine editor, as a self-proclaimed figurehead of the *Aesthetic Movement*, as a poet, as a conversationalist, as a homosexual, queer or—if you like—bisexual, as an Irishman rather than an Englishman, as a playwright, a convicted criminal and champion of prison reform, and so on.

Despite all these separate thematic perspectives, several new complete biographies have appeared in recent years, that attempt to bring all Wilde's sometimes contradictory sub-personalities together in one composite portrait. This is the more admirable, at a time, more than a century after the writer's death, when there are hardly any new biographical facts or archival documents to be brought to light.

The biography simply titled *Oscar Wilde* (1987), by the literary scholar and previously Joyce- and Yeats-biographer Richard Ellmann, is considered by many to be the best modern life of the author, as such the successor to the masterful *The Life of Oscar Wilde*, published in 1946 by Hesketh Pearson. Indeed, Ellmann's book is impressive in style, composition, and feeling for the subject, but it is unfortunately marred by so many errors that its usefulness as a source is seriously limited. The German cultural historian Horst Schroeder tolerated Ellmann's sloppiness so badly that he compiled a publication entitled *Additions and Corrections to Richard Ellmann's Oscar Wilde,* the last edition of which (2002) runs to more than 300 pages.

To give a single example out of many of the type of carelessness with the facts that the reader of Ellmann's biography must deal with: Ellmann mentions that Oscar Wilde met and fell in love with a seventeen-year-old girl in August 1875 and that she lived with her parents in Dublin at 1 Marion Terrace. Almost everything in this simple statement is incorrect. Wilde did not meet this girl until a year later, in the summer of 1876, when she was eighteen (not seventeen), and she lived with her parents not at 1, Marion Terrace, but at 1, Marino Crescent. Are such small factual errors important? For the book you are presently reading, in any case, they are quite crucial, because it was at this particular address that much of the story of the golden crucifix took place.

As a matter of fact, it is this very period in Wilde's life that fascinates me most: the time of his studies at Oxford (from October 1874) until his move to London (in December 1878), when he began his literary-journalistic career. These are the years, in his early twenties, that all his intellectual, creative and social talents begin to blossom. He excels in Greek language and literature, comes under the influence of great minds such as John Ruskin and Walter Pater; makes friends and engages in energetic correspondence with his fellow students; wins an important academic poetry prize with a long poem (*Ravenna*, 1878), and he falls in love, not once but many times. In love with classical antiquity, most of all with Greece; in love with the fragrant and lavish rituals of the Roman Catholic Church and with Italy; in love with the painting and architecture of the Renaissance; and—last but not least—he falls in love with a girl, a girl from Dublin, since of course these are also the years of his life that he starts to lead a sexually active life as a young man.

That girl's name was Florence Balcombe. Wilde courted her, wrote poems for her, drew her portrait, they exchanged love letters, and on Christmas Day 1876, the young couple went together in Dublin to the Christmas Service at St. Patrick's, the cathedral of which Jonathan Swift was once Dean. Or was it Christchurch Cathedral where they went? On that point, the different biographies vary. Anyway, to seal their love on that day, Oscar gave Florence a small golden crucifix, in which he had their names or initials engraved for eternity. Or just his own; there is no certainty about that either. In any case, the gift of this little piece of jewellery is a gesture, as many young lovers make, a gesture expected to give a perpetuating power to a budding and still immature love affair.

In each life things go wrong, and many things that at first seem to be self-evident, at a later stage turn out to be completely untenable. Oscar Wilde is a particularly poignant

Portrait of Florence Balcombe drawn by Oscar Wilde in 1877

example of this truth, but it also applies to Florence Balcombe, who almost two years later, on the 4th of December, 1878, quite suddenly married a young court clerk from Dublin. This civil servant was also an ambitious, budding writer, with a great interest in the theatre. Bram Stoker was his name, and he would later gain literary recognition and popular renown with the novel *Dracula*, which after the author's death would even become a classic of the horror-genre. It is no great exaggeration to speak of the relationship between these two writers and the girl they both loved as a love triangle. A rather sinister triangle, as will be seen, in which hidden forces and meanings were at work.

After all these years of reading Oscar Wilde, writing about him, translating him, and collecting him, this book finally found its decisive direction in an almost accidental way. I remember the moment crystal clear: I had just stepped out of the shower, and while I was trying to recall the young Florence Balcombe and wondering how her change of heart from Oscar Wilde to Bram Stoker had exactly occurred, I suddenly saw the following question lying around in a corner of my mind, as it were, a question that has not left me since: where would that little golden crucifix have gone, which Oscar Wilde gave as a gift to—then—'his' girl on the 25th of December, 1876?

3

GREECE

What was on the mind of the twenty-two-year-old student Oscar Wilde in the months after he had presented the little golden cross as a seasonal love gift to Florence Balcombe? He spent the remaining weeks of his Christmas holiday in Dublin with his mother at his parents' house in Merrion Square; he made the social rounds of evening parties at the houses of befriended families; he attended a theatre performance by the great actor Henry Irving and went to a concert of Haydn's *The Creation*. Even after returning to Oxford, as soon as the holidays were over, he spent his time not so much studying as visiting exhibitions in London and decorating his new rooms at Magdalen College, which he had taken over from his college friend William Ward, overlooking the river Cherwell. Already in those years he devoted a lot of energy to keeping up his friendly correspondences.

While we assume that the golden crucifix hung around Florence Balcombe's neck all this time, Oscar was busy planning a trip to the South in the spring of 1877. Rome was his goal, mainly because of the city's Catholic associations, but with characteristic fickleness he allowed himself to be persuaded by

Oscar Wilde as a student in Oxford, spring 1876

his former tutor at Trinity College Dublin, the classicist John Pentland Mahaffy, to turn to Brindisi instead. From there he travelled with Mahaffy as tour guide and in the company of two other students to the country that competed with the world of the Roman Catholic faith for the favours of his inquisitive spirit. In particular it was Mahaffy who, by immersing him in the pagan culture of classical Greece, wanted to cure the young, somewhat bigoted Oscar of his 'Romish leanings.'

In short, it was to be a decisive adventure in his younger life, and wouldn't it be nice to be able to follow him step by step on this journey, in order to get a clearer picture of his adventures and his state of mind at the time? In the absence of a well-functioning time machine and since film as a medium would not be invented until almost twenty years later, there are in theory two sources for such a travelogue. The most obvious possibility would be that Wilde himself had written about his Greek journey. Given the deep impression that this three-week tour of the Peloponnese must have made on him, there would have been every reason for him to do so. Moreover, in his student years, Wilde not only kept a commonplace book, to jot down favourite quotes and excerpts from authors he was reading, but also a notebook with his own thoughts. Together, these two cahiers give a unique picture of what he read and thought in those years and what ideas and observations he derived from the lessons he took in the fields of classical literature, ancient history and ancient philosophy. Unfortunately, these two notebooks hardly contain any trace of his Greek journey.

His father, the Irish eye and ear surgeon Sir William Wilde, made more of a similar journey he undertook in his younger years. In 1844 he published a detailed account of his grand tour six years earlier under the title: *Narrative of a Voyage to Madeira, Teneriffe and Along the Shores of the Mediterranean, Including a Visit to Algiers, Egypt, Palestine, Tyre, Rhodes, Telmessus, Cyprus and Greece*. In the latter country—by then we are already well past page 500—the reader will find beautiful descriptions of a still undersized Athens (in previous years it has grown into a city of no less than 20,000 inhabitants!), including trips to the Plain of Marathon, Argos, Tiryns and Mycenae, the same places that his son Oscar would also visit more than thirty years later.

Oscar Wilde's twenty-three-year-old father-to-be travels through Greece during Orthodox Easter Week and witnesses impressive religious ceremonies with burning torches and nocturnal processions of priests and soldiers. Regarding the traditional burial of the host, he writes: 'a scene of greater violence and confusion can scarcely be imagined among a people calling themselves Christian.' The discharging of firearms on the morning of Easter Sunday, which Wilde Sr. describes as quite an odd way of expressing joy at the resurrection of Jesus Christ, had probably much to do with the Greeks' recent victory over the Ottomans in their War of Independence. After travelling around Greek territory for almost three weeks, Wilde *père* set sail for home again via Gibraltar.

From his son Oscar, however, no more than a few letters and a few loose notes about his Greek journey have survived. After his return, he gave a lecture under the title *Hellenism*, but it is hardly clear from the text that he himself had recently visited the country extensively. Of the other writing plans he refers to in his correspondence, nothing materialised. Perhaps the experience was too overwhelming, or were there too many other pursuits and interests that demanded his attention immediately after his return? After all, he was twenty-two, and that is not an age for dwelling long on any kind of experience, but rather for pursuing new ones.

The second possible source for an impression of Oscar Wilde during his trip through Greece in the spring of 1877 would be a report written by one of his travel companions. That seems logical, at a time when a trip to and through Greece, especially under the guidance of such an authority as Mahaffy, was still a precious rarity. George Augustin Macmillan, who was one year younger than Oscar Wilde, did indeed write an account of their journey together and published the result a year after their return under the title "A Ride Across the Peloponnese" in *Blackwood's Edinburgh Magazine*. For Macmillan, who went straight from Eton to the publishing house Macmillan, founded in 1843 by his father and an uncle, his affinity for Greece would soon become even more clear by his becoming one of the founders of the English *Society for the Promotion of Hellenic Studies*. Unfortunately, Macmillan hardly sketches any personal portraits of his travel companions, and our curiosity about the young Oscar Wilde and his experiences on the road is not really satisfied by this account.

For inspirer and tour guide Mahaffy himself, this trip provided an occasion to supplement the next edition of his book *Rambles and Studies in Greece* (1876), with a number of new experiences during the journey undertaken in 1877. Through his picturesque and detailed observations, we sometimes come close to the person of the young Oscar Wilde, at the table in a Greek inn, trotting on horseback through the Arcadian landscape or clambering over the remains of an ancient castle. But it all remains hazy, and the simple 'who is who' in these travel notes can only be based on guesswork.

Our last hope is pinned on Cambridge student William Goulding, who completes the travelling foursome. He was the twenty-one-year-old son of a well-to-do Irish businessman, and after completing his studies at St. John College would go on to work for the family business in fertilisers and phosphates. He was not a very intellectually inclined boy. In a letter to his own father, George Macmillan even calls him 'delightfully innocent of what we call culture,' but he must have been ok as a travelling companion, and in Cambridge he undoubtedly received a fine education. And, not unimportantly, it was his father who was sponsoring the trip and paying Mahaffy to enlighten his son during this Easter holiday journey to

Greece. For young Goulding it was even the second of such a Mediterranean journey with Mahaffy.

Maybe we should just grab this last straw and imagine that William Goulding wrote a letter to his father on his way back from Athens. The longer I ponder the probability of the existence of such a letter, the more certain I am of how the text might have read.

4

FOOTSTEPS

To W. Goulding, Esq.
Summerhill House
County Cork, Ireland

On board S.S. Massilia, 17 April 1877

Dear Father,

These past few days in Athens we have been so busy with our last viewings and visits that I am only now able to keep my promise and write to you about the continuation of our journey. Just before we embarked from Brindisi a fortnight ago on the S.S. Trinacria in the direction of Zante and Corfu, I posted an earlier letter to you, which should have reached you by now. In the meantime, I hope that you and Mama are doing well, and that the spring weather is conducive to both your health. Here the air already feels very much like summer, especially in the wide openness on board this passenger boat of the Messageries Maritimes, which will take us in less than two days to Naples. This gives me every opportunity to collect some more of my travel impressions for you in a letter, which I will post at the Neapolitan port office upon our arrival.

Although this fairly new French ship, on which we left Piraeus yesterday afternoon, is fully booked, we have no complaints about the service and the facilities on board. Our first-class cabins are not very large, but in their simplicity comfortable enough. In the morning at about 9 o'clock, a three-course breakfast is served, in which the sheep's cheese and the olives merit a special mention.

As I wrote to you in the P.S. under my previous letter, since Genoa there are no longer three of us, but four, now that another former student of Professor Mahaffy has joined our party. His name is Oscar Wilde. He exchanged Trinity College Dublin a few years ago for Magdalen College, Oxford, but Mahaffy still considers him his student, and apparently Wilde sees it that way too. Two years ago, I met him during my previous Mediterranean trip in Florence. Since then he has become even more confident than he already was, and has noticeably expanded his knowledge in art, literature, and history. The discussions between him and Professor Mahaffy are often very worthwhile to listen to. Sometimes they even play out verbal duels with quotes in ancient Greek.

This second full day of our crossing most passengers spend in peace, sitting on deck, talking, reading or looking out over the sea. As I write, I am sitting in a small saloon on the upper deck, where

*every now and then a passenger steps in to smoke a
cigarette out of the wind, to which I have no objection. This small saloon is a perfect writing room,
with a completely unobstructed view to the left and
to the right, or as I should of course say: to port
and to starboard. Diagonally across from me in this
room is a black piano. Fortunately, it is not used
by anyone. When I peer out over the flat seawater
from the side window here, I sometimes feel as if I
can already make out a coastline in the distance, but
this then turns out to be an illusion of the horizon. I
benefit a lot from the glasses with smoke-coloured
lenses that I bought in Brindisi, because in April the
sunlight here is already very bright, especially if
reflected by the water.*

*Just like two years ago, you have done me a great
pleasure, Father, by making this journey possible.
Professor Mahaffy is once again a capital teacher,
combining a great knowledge of history in many fields,
with the ability to evoke the past in conversations in
such a way that it truly comes to life. Together with
George Macmillan, about whom I wrote to you in
detail earlier, we form a close-knit group of travellers,
since our arrival in Greece on 4 April in the port of
Katakolon, on the west coast of the Peloponnese. That
arrival, at nightfall, was a solemn moment, even for
those of us who had previously set foot on Greek soil.
All four of us stood silently at the railing of the boat
that slowly approached the coastal town and then
slipped into the harbour, while behind us the sun set in
burning colours, a magical experience.*

The next morning, when we were on our way by carriage to the city of Pyrgos, Oscar Wilde had me read a poem he had written the previous night about our arrival on the Greek mainland. I cannot quote it from memory, except for the last line, which read: 'I stood upon the strand of Greece at last!' Even if for me it was the second time I arrived in Greece, I too experienced that triumphant feeling again, although of most Greek glory mere ruins and fragments remain, surrounded by market towns and mountain villages, and instead of heroes and gods, the country is now mainly inhabited by merchants, shepherds and donkey drivers. According to Wilde, with whom I spoke about it on the way in the carriage in response to his poem, a confrontation with the real Greece is a 'combination of the tangible and the unattainable,' as he called it. We were able to test his opinion during our visit to the excavations in Olympia.

First, I should mention that when we left the island of Zante, we were joined by the archaeologist Dr Hirschfeld from Koenigsberg. He is the one in charge of the excavations that have been taking place in Olympia since last year. It was therefore a privilege to be able to visit the site the next day, not only together with Professor Mahaffy but also in the company of this German colleague of his. However, the first sight of the famous holy place was something of a shock. Instead of a serene complex of ruined shrines, as I had expected to find, we saw enormous devastation caused by the passage of so many centuries, by past earthquakes and by the ongoing excavations. Sand piles could be seen everywhere, there were wheelbarrows and wooden carts and scaffolding had been built and tarpaulins stretched to protect the finds and the workers from the sunlight and possible rain.

The shock of this chaotic sight was more than made up for by several startling finds that we were allowed to see, in particular the sculpture of a victory goddess, which was excavated there last December. The face of this Statue of Victory has unfortunately been violated, yet you can easily imagine the impression that this winged white marble victory goddess must once have made on visitors to the sanctuary, especially when Dr Hirschfeld told us that in ancient times in the temple of Hera this statue probably looked down on the people from a high position.

While we were in a small barn next to the over-turned excavation site to view the battered figure, Professor Mahaffy came back to our earlier conversation on the way to Pyrgos. According to Mahaffy, it is precisely archaeology that forms a connection between the literature and historiography of Greece on the one hand and the historical and cultural imagination with which we look at that civilisation on the other. Therefore, he believes, archaeologists should not rebuild or restore what has been damaged by time. According to him, this would but detract from the imagination that later generations have to muster themselves in order to do justice to the past.

The fact that the drums of the many temple columns, instead of being stacked vertically on top of each other, are now scattered horizontally like thick slabs in rows on the grass, gave me the feeling of witnessing an area hit by disaster, such as the explosion of a powder magazine. At the same time, it was wonderfully quiet there, with only the chirping sound of the cicadas in the tall grass and in the sparse pine trees, mingled with the muffled knocking and the voices of the many dozens of workers digging around the site.

Professor Mahaffy and Dr Hirschfeld had a lot to discuss with each other about the significance and further destination of the finds made, so we students were left to ourselves for a few hours. The three of us walked around on our own, listening to the flow of words from our new travel companion Oscar Wilde, who at one moment had a theory about the silver underside of olive leaves, while the next he praised the seemingly weightless and spiritual qualities of the marble that the Greeks used for their statues. I have already said that his language is quite artful, and with all his artistic ideas he sometimes rivals Professor Mahaffy in conversational talent. He regularly quotes ancient writers in the original Greek, and also knows many poems by Shelley, Keats and Swinburne by heart.

That same evening, we sat down to a meal in a neighbouring mountain village called Drouva, where we were served a delicious roasted lamb in a small inn, accompanied by a white wine that tasted so much like resin that it was more like a kind of liquid wax. Looking back on the impressive day we had behind us, we listened to the stories of Professor Mahaffy. In particular, I remember an anecdote he told about the historian Thucydides, who as a fourteen-year-old boy had travelled to Olympia specifically to listen to the great Herodotus who was invited there to read from his own writings. To think, Father, that I too have walked there now, and that I may have sat on the very same stone bench on which young Thucydides sat listening to his great teacher!

While we were discussing our travel plans for the next day, it struck me that still no railway lines have been built anywhere in the Peloponnese. Our conversation led Oscar Wilde to an opinion, which he defended with great passion, that the construction of railways in a country has no less mental influence on the population than the work of thinkers like Luther or Voltaire. Professor Mahaffy thought the comparison was too far-fetched, but it certainly made for a lively and entertaining table conversation.

From Drouva the next morning we rode on horseback along the banks of the river Alpheios in the direction of Andritsaena, from where we would visit another highlight, the Apollo Temple of Bassae. We left the province of Elis and entered Arcadia, which has the name of being lovely and pastoral, but whose mountainous nature with its many rugged hills and rock formations has a rather difficult character for the traveller. Thanks to our guide Nicholas, whose services Professor Mahaffy had engaged on our arrival in Katakolon, we managed to reach our destination in one long day, driving through flowering landscapes with fruit trees and thorny shrubs. Even though you just sit on a horse, due to the constant movement and the fact that you have to keep your balance all the time, especially when it goes uphill or downhill, this mode of travelling is more exhausting than I expected. In the perched mountain village of Andritsaena the facilities were extremely modest—all four of us had to sleep in one sparsely furnished room—but a few blankets spread out on the floor were sufficient to me for a good night's rest.

The next day it rained hard, but even so our visit to the temple of Bassae was an unforgettable experience. Father, imagine a temple like the Parthenon on the Athenian Acropolis, erected in the desolation of a plateau, as rocky as it is barren and uncultivated. The temple is not made of marble but of a pale-grey slate, exactly the same colour as the surrounding mountain landscape, so that the monumental building is, as it were, incorporated into the surrounding terrain, as if it arose naturally out of it as an organism, as Oscar Wilde put it. It is no coincidence that this Apollo temple was built by the same architect as the Parthenon, and both buildings, despite the great differences in location and material, are well-matched in beauty and stark superiority.

On returning to Andritsaena in the evening, it had become too late to travel on to our next staging point, so we had to spend an extra night on our blankets in the meagre room. During a late evening walk after dinner, out of curiosity we entered a local church, where a Greek Orthodox Easter Mass was being celebrated. Professor Mahaffy did not last long, and despite our genuine interest, the thick air of incense and burning candles was soon too much for Macmillan and me as well. Wilde stayed on a little longer and later claimed that he had undergone the Mass as a particularly meaningful ceremony, precisely because he could not understand a word of it. As I said, he sometimes has strange ideas.

This was also evident the next day, when Professor Mahaffy, at our simple breakfast of sheep's cheese, milk and bread, questioned some miracles from the Christian Bible, and contrasted them with the mythological stories of the gods of Ancient Greece. The turning of water into wine cannot be regarded as historical fact, he contended, no more than the birth of Pallas Athene from the head of Zeus. Wilde insisted, against the protests of the three of us, that turning water into wine was not at all unthinkable. He professed that miracles are just another aspect of all the phenomena that nature consists of. George Macmillan half-seriously assumed that Wilde had probably lingered too long in the Greek Orthodox church the previous evening to speak rationally on this subject.

After an interruption of a few hours, I hereby continue my travelogue. The early part of our boat trip from Piraeus was rather smooth, but then we were surprised by stormy weather and sturdy waves, which at first made walking and writing difficult and then left the four of us quite shaken. Even lying down did not prevent most passengers from becoming sick. Now, the sky is still cloudy, but it has stopped raining, and the *sea is gradually calming down again. I hope that we can continue our journey in this reasonable stillness, although at this time in spring one can apparently not be entirely sure.*

Following our departure from Andritsaena we crossed the interior of the Peloponnese via Megalopolis and Tripolis on horseback again. This happened at a rather slow pace, for the simple reason that our guide Nicholas often took the horses by the hand, especially over mountain passes, at fords in rivers or during otherwise difficult parts of our route. Each time Professor Mahaffy attempted to encourage the horses to a somewhat higher pace, our guide protested loudly, so we had to accept our slow advance. In the meantime, we enjoyed the beautiful and varied spring landscape around us.

Near Tripolis we visited the remains of the Athena temple in Tegea. Hardly any archaeological excavations have so far been carried out there, which may be why the impression of these scattered remains was all the more overwhelming. It felt as if no one had been here in ages, and I even began to doubt the need to dig up and upend everything in this country. Instead of honouring the past everywhere, this newly independent nation could also choose to focus on the future and provide its population with more of the modern conveniences and amenities that industrial development has brought us.

With that we had almost reached the southeast coast of the Peloponnese. That we had been mercilessly overcharged by our innkeeper in Tripolis, that there

*was all too frequent cause for arguing with our guide
and that we were almost robbed on the final stretch of
our journey over land, all this was quickly forgotten
at the sight of the remains of the large amphitheatre
in Argos, followed by our visit to Mycenae, the city
of Agamemnon, where Dr Schliemann is busy with
his excavations. Unfortunately, the great scholar
and writer himself was not present at the time of our
visit, for I would have gladly shaken hands with the
discoverer of Troy, who is a personal acquaintance of
Professor Mahaffy.*

*Our visit was nevertheless very impressive. My
preliminary reading had not prepared me for the
beautiful location of the Mycenaean citadel, both in
terms of landscape and of military advantage. The
situation of the fortress of Tiryns was less grand,
merely in the flat landscape, a stone's throw from the
dirt road that runs from Argos to the North, but that
was offset by the most impenetrable walls I have ever
seen. According to the guard on duty the walls in most
places have a thickness of up to twenty-six feet. For
this reason alone, Tiryns in my view should be added
to the seven wonders of the ancient world.*

*And so, dear Father, we arrived at the Mediterra-
nean coast and from the port town of Nea-Epidavros
reached the Greek capital Athens by boat via the island
of Aegina on 12 April. There, as a reward, the many
beauties already known to me from my first visit
awaited the four of us. On a visit to the vaults of the
Greek National Bank, we were also allowed, through
the connections of Professor Mahaffy, to admire the*

treasures that the recent archaeological expeditions in Mycenae have brought to light. Amid those finds, Agamemnon's death mask was certainly the most magnificent one. I was able to buy a picture of it, which I will gladly show you, because it is really like looking the Homeric king straight in the face from a distance of so many centuries.

Another wonderful experience was the visit we made to the battlefield at Marathon, where the Greeks defeated the Persians 2500 years ago. It was a bright and beautiful spring day, peaceful and serene, the complete opposite of the clatter of arms and soldiers' cries that have given that plain its bloody place in the history books.

While Professor Mahaffy and Macmillan went to an appointment with the British consul, I spent the last morning of our three-day stay in Athens with Wilde. He had himself portrayed in a photo studio, dressed for the occasion in traditional Greek costume. That was more to his taste than to mine. At the post office it turned out that there was a card from his fiancée for him. He was exceptionally delighted and walked about with it as if he had won a prize. Then he and I took a walk all the way around the Acropolis, past Herod's theatre and the Olympieion, until at the foot of that huge rock we unexpectedly came upon a little cemetery with an adjacent small church. On the domed roof was an excessively large cross that shone brightly in the sunlight, and as traces of the recent Easter festivities many flowers were attached to the windows and to the open door of the chapel.

Oscar Wilde in Athens during his Greek trip in 1877

The timeless intimacy of this modest Christian sanctuary made quite an impression on both of us, and—without telling Professor Mahaffy, who does not appreciate such expressions of religious belief—we both lit a candle inside the church, at which I silently formulated a benediction for my loved ones. 'Everything,' Oscar Wilde claimed as we continued our walk moments later, 'ultimately comes down to imagination.' According to him, imagination is the only possible connection between the God of nature and the God of conscience.

Be that as it may, it looks like we will arrive at the port of Naples early tomorrow morning. This evening the Sicilian coast is passing us by to starboard and in a few hours' time we will sail through the Strait of Messina. I hope to see everyone back in good health before very long, as soon as I can come to Dublin to tell you about all the rest of my travel impressions.

For now, with much love for both of you, and also with a personal greeting on behalf of Professor Mahaffy, I sign, your loving son,

William

5

STUDENT

E xactly one hundred years after Oscar Wilde, in the summer of 1977, I set foot myself for the first time on Greek
soil. The 'I stood upon the strand of Greece at last'-sensation
was indeed overwhelming, after five years of Greek lessons
in secondary school and as a student in Leiden absorbed in a
course of Greek Papyrology. Every fresh Greek traveller, who
until then has gained his knowledge of the country mainly by
reading ancient Greek texts, awaits the same process of mental
transformation from booklore to actual physical experience.

Right from 1871, when Wilde entered Trinity College
Dublin, he was immersed in the field of ancient literature
and history. Iain Ross, who wrote his PhD thesis on Wilde's relationship to the world of classical Greece (*Oscar Wilde
and Ancient Greece*, 2013), has dug up what students in their
first and second year at Trinity were supposed to master at
that time. This involved both a required reading of historical and literary studies, making translations (partly prepared,
partly *a prima vista*) and above all a corpus of authors that the
students had to be thoroughly familiar with: Demosthenes,
Euripides and Herodotus in the first year, Plato, Sophocles,

Homer, Thucydides, Aischines and Isocrates in the second. Examinations were both written and oral.

The young Oscar performed well above the average in these assignments. In February 1874 he even won the Berkeley Gold Medal for Greek, in a competition on the fragments of the Greek comic poets, as collected in a seven-volume edition by the German classicist and Menander-specialist Augustus Meineke. That hefty slice of gold, provided with a motto derived from Homer's *Iliad*: AIEN APIΣTEYEIN ('Always excel'), was one of two annual awards, established by the eighteenth-century Anglican bishop and former Trinity-fellow George Berkeley to encourage the study of Greek. The medal carried considerable academic and intellectual prestige and with its 18-karat gold it was also an object of significant value.

It is no wonder that, as a talented student, Wilde drew special attention from his teachers, in particular from Mahaffy, for whom he worked as an editorial assistant. In the preface to *Social Life in Greece from Homer to Menander* (1874), Mahaffy thanked his student by name for the 'improvements and corrections all through the book.'

Unfortunately, when it comes to the ancient Greek Eros, which traditionally holds a special place for the beauty and physical attractiveness of young boys, Mahaffy was quite prudish. Iain Ross characterises Mahaffy's treatment of this subject as a combination of 'puritanism, sentimentality and innocence bordering on imbecility.' For example, the author maintains on rather vague grounds that in the Greek worship of boys, romantic and chivalrous feelings were more important than the sexual component. It is not for nothing that Oscar Wilde and his professor would grow apart in future years: Wilde wrote a scathing review of one of Mahaffy's later studies (*Greek Life and Thought*, 1887) and Mahaffy, for his part, refused to sign a petition calling for the early release of the imprisoned Wilde, calling him 'the only blot' on his career as an academic tutor.

In the mid-1870s everything was still hand and glove between the Irish historian and his brilliant student, and it was only thanks to Wilde's exceptional academic achievements that continuing his education at prestigious Oxford seemed more obvious than staying on in Dublin. On the 23rd of June, 1874, he successfully passed an entrance exam, securing a scholarship of £95 per year for five years.

Although Wilde excelled at the linguistic level and at making translations, under the influence of Mahaffy he increasingly preferred the visual dimension, the history, the imagination, the artistic and the human aspect and above all the beauty of all that was Greek. The academy of Wilde's era was greatly influenced by the new science of archeology, with finds so spectacular and inescapable that classicists and ancient historians could not ignore them.

Apart from the *Nike* of Paeionios, the battered statue of the victory goddess that our four travellers were allowed to admire in Olympia, in that same spring of 1877 the German archaeologist Ernst Curtius pulled out from the ruins of what had once been the temple of Hera the marble Hermes statue by the Greek sculptor Praxiteles. Until then, the existence of the statue was known only from a brief reference to it in the guide to Greece written by the geographer Pausanias in the second century AD.

After returning from his Greek trip, Oscar Wilde told anyone who wanted to listen in rhapsodic terms about the thrill of seeing with his own eyes the marble god being liberated from the earth that had covered him for so many centuries. He praised 'the beauty and transparency of the marble,' compared it to 'sunlit ivory,' and in later years even purchased a plaster replica of the statue, which was given a prominent place on the mantelpiece of his study in Tite Street.

An ever so slight, but annoying detail in this story, is that Oscar Wilde and his three companions visited Olympia in the first week of April 1877, while the Hermes of Praxiteles was only brought to light there on May 7 of that year, so that he could not possibly have witnessed the actual excavation. In his life's philosophy this was probably just a minor correction to historical reality, which merely served to make the truth stand out all the more beautifully.

Something Oscar Wilde and his fellow travellers undoubtedly saw with their own eyes in Athens was the golden death mask of a Mycenaean king excavated by Heinrich Schliemann. Schliemann assumed that this was the mask of Agamemnon and, after his discovery on the 28th of November, 1876, he sent the legendary telegram to the Greek King George I: 'Your Majesty, I have gazed on the face of Agamemnon.' Legendary indeed, because as David Traill has shown in his debunking Schliemann-biography (*Schliemann of Troy: Treasure and Deceit,* 1995), such a telegram was never sent at all. Moreover, the death mask was not of Agamemnon, but of his father Atreus. Even if you intend to stick to the historical facts, you still have to avoid constantly tripping over the historical remnants of earlier fantasy stories.

What is indisputable, is that during his stay in Athens Oscar Wilde had himself portrayed in traditional Greek costume by the society photographer Petros Moraitis. An original of this cabinet photo is in the collection of the British Museum, but perhaps Moraitis made several original prints. The fake rock formation on which Wilde has placed his impressively booted right foot is identical to that in many other portraits from Moraitis' studio on Odos Aiolou no. 82, so that the authenticity of the portrait need not be doubted.

After the famous photograph of Oscar Wilde as a toddler at the age of two or three, as depicted in many biographies, this was the second time in his life that he posed for a photographer in a dress, with the understanding that this of course is not a real dress, but the national costume of the *evzones*, the elite corps of the royal bodyguard. The cotton white men's skirt is called a *fustanella* in Greek. Apparently, photographer Moraitis had an extensive dress-up box in his studio, because on many websites of dealers in historical photographs and elsewhere on the internet you can find all kinds of outfits and attributes with which people have been immortalised in his studio, including musical instruments, rifles, and scimitars. For his customers the fact that Moraitis also counted members of the Greek Royal Family among his clientele was probably an added attraction.

Petros Moraitis did not just work as a portrait photographer, he also photographed cityscapes that capture the attraction of travel in Greece at the time. A series of albumen prints from the 1870s that I found on the auction site Catawiki, show how cleverly Moraitis responded to the tourist market. A shot of the Parthenon from the southeast shows the temple of the Olympian Zeus, the Olympieion, once the largest ancient temple in all of Greece, at that time not yet encroached upon by surrounding modern buildings. Everything, even in the distance, is razor sharp: the fluting of the

Corinthian columns, the succulents and cypresses, even the leaves of the olive trees on the right, as well as the shutters of a few dilapidated houses that stand somewhat in the distance at the foot of the Acropolis.

Far back in the left of this photograph you can just make out two men on wooden chairs under a ramshackle shelter. Nearby, a dog is sleeping in the shade. No one can say for certain who are these two men under that roof, perhaps catching their breath after a joint walk around the Acropolis in the heat of the sun, so why couldn't they be our two students Oscar Wilde and William Goulding?

During all those walks through the Greek capital, Oscar must have carried in his pocket the sweet Easter-postcard that Florence Balcombe had sent him *poste restante* to Athens. An answer from him to that card has not survived and the golden cross that hung around his girl's neck in faraway Dublin seems to be as far away from our grasp as ever. Perhaps biographical research is unsuited for finding a lost piece of jewellery after almost a century and a half. Wouldn't it be much more effective to simply call in a detective?

6

GOLD RUSH

What would have happened to the Berkeley Gold Medal, which Oscar Wilde won in his second year at Trinity for his achievements in Greek? In no biography have I ever come across a mention of the present whereabouts of this medal, two of which were given out by this Irish university every year from 1752 onwards. The thing does come up at least once in every biography, and often more, because in times of penury Wilde repeatedly used it as collateral for money loans, and happily got it back afterwards. Biographer Matthew Sturgis, for example, writes of the medal: 'It would be a lasting and material memento of Wilde's time at Trinity.' Sure, but where is it?

Since the name of the winner was not engraved in the medal, it would not be easy to determine whether a copy was indeed that of Oscar Wilde. Could DNA-research on the surface of the medal offer any degree of certainty? Every now and then, one pops up in an auction, but as much as the writer is close to my heart, it would be madness to try and buy them all, hoping that one of them on further investigation will turn out to be a trophy for my Wilde-collection. Moreover, it is not one of the two Berkeley Gold Medals for Greek from 1874 that I am obsessed with, but the little golden crucifix that the infatuated Oscar gave to his girlfriend two years later. One gold rush at a time.

To complicate matters further, at this stage of Wilde's life there is even a third golden object, a jewel that has left a thriller-like trail over the years. Like with the vanished crucifix, that history begins in December 1876, when twenty-two-year-old Oscar Wilde, together with his slightly younger fellow-student Reginald Harding, presented a golden friendship ring to their mutual college friend William Ward. The ring was given in honour of the latter's graduation, shortly before he left on a five-month journey across Europe.

This 18-karat gold friendship ring had quite a remarkable design of a belt closed with a buckle. On the outside was the engraved inscription in Greek: Μνημόσυνον φιλίας ἀντιφιλοῦντι φίλοι ('A memento of the reciprocal friendship between two friends and a friend') and on the inside was engraved: 'OFOFWW & RRH to WWW, 1876' (i.e. Oscar Fingal O'Flahertie Wills Wilde & Richard Reginald Harding to William Welsford Ward, 1876). In later life, Ward, who had become a lawyer in Bristol, donated the ring, along with several letters from Wilde in their student days, to Magdalen College. The university included these items in its historical collection and showed some of them in a permanent exhibition, in memory of their formerly controversial, but now world-famous alumnus. It is from here that the wanderings of this golden jewel commence.

To begin with, on the 2nd of May 2002, the ring was stolen together with some university rowing medals from a display case in the library of Magdalen College by one

Eamonn Andrews, formerly employed as a cleaner and handyman in the building. Before he gained access to the library, the intruder first thoroughly feasted on the whisky stock of the college bar, after which he injured himself when breaking the glass of the display case. Unaware of its intrinsic and historical value, he sold the ring to a dealer in scrap metal for just £150, whereas it was insured for £35,000. Thanks to the blood traces left on shards of the broken glass the thief was quickly identified and sentenced to two years in prison just months later. It was not his first crime; he still had to serve a much longer prison sentence, that had remained outstanding after a previous conviction. But that did not bring the ring back.

To the chagrin of Magdalen College and many Oscar Wilde admirers, the writer's golden relic remained untraceable, and with the passing of the years, it was feared that the thing had been melted down. Until a second theft took place, a rather more spectacular one. In fact, it was the largest burglary ever committed in England and by comparison it completely dwarfs the earlier petty break-in at Oxford.

On Thursday the 2nd of April 2015 at 9:19pm, the staff of the London firm of Hatton Garden Safety Deposit Ltd is closing up the office for the long Easter weekend. The company, owned by a Sudanese family, is located in the middle of the capital's diamond centre, on the edge of the Holborn District, home to about sixty jewellery stores and some three hundred offices trading in precious metals and stones.

In its high-security cellars Hatton Garden Safety Deposit, located at the corner of Hatton Garden and Greville Street, contains no less than 999 safe-deposit boxes, rented out to wealthy individuals, jewellers and other dealers in valuables. The heavy, jet-black front door, reinforced with shiny polished copper strips, gives an impression of the luxury trade of the various companies established in this building.

Minutes after the office is locked on that Thursday night, a red-haired man with a key to the front door enters the building. He in turn opens the fire exit around the corner on Greville Street to half a dozen men, dressed in conspicuous workwear and wearing yellow construction helmets. On surveillance camera footage the word GAS can be seen on the back of one of the men's vests, but none of the six faces comes recognisably into view. And the men are definitely not going to concern themselves with the gas piping.

From a white van, they bring the necessary items into the building, including two mobile waste bins and a Hilti DD350 diamond drilling machine. On the British website of this drill manufacturer, the recommendation for the device reads: 'For a quick performance boost with increased torque when drilling through rebar.' A drill of this type nowadays costs £8,000. No child's toy, then.

Remarkably, all the men are in their sixties and seventies, each one with an entire career in crime behind him. Their leader is seventy-six-year-old Brian Reader, who received his first burglary conviction back in 1950, when he was eleven years old. Together, the men have spent three years discussing the preparation and organisation of their plans during regular meetings on Friday nights in a pub called The Castle on Pentonville Road in Islington. One more big hit, and then retirement, that was the idea from the beginning.

Once inside the building, the men send the lift to the second floor and hang a sign OUT OF SERVICE at the lift doors, so that they can descend through the lift shafts to the basement. After disabling the alarm system equipped with motion sensors and forcing a metal gate, they start their intensive drilling job, straight through a reinforced concrete wall 20 inches thick, to the neighbouring room where the lockers are located.

What the men did not take into account is that the alarm system automatically sends a text message the moment the device is deactivated. Thus, at 12:21am the owner of the safe deposit company, who is in Sudan at the time, receives a call that his alarm system has gone off. He is—as it turns out wrongly—informed that the police will arrive on the scene. Since the alarm had recently gone off accidentally as a result of an insect flying around in the basement, the notification does not cause great concern or action. On the contrary. An hour later, a security guard walks around the building, inspecting the front door and looking in through the fire exit letterbox. He sees nothing untoward, concludes that the alarm was false and leaves again, without entering the building. His work instruction entails that after an alarm he is under no circumstances to enter a building without police escort. The police did also receive an automatic alarm signal, but this was not acted upon, for which the police authorities will later publicly offer apologies. Perhaps their laxness had also to do with a power outage because of an underground fire in the neighbourhood, which in the past few days caused many of the surrounding buildings to experience power supply failures, a fortuitous coincidence for the burglars.

So, the men continue their work unhindered until early Saturday morning, when their drilling is obstructed by the back of a locker wall anchored in the floor and the ceiling.

With the hydraulic ram they brought, there is no getting through this. So shortly after 8am on Saturday morning the men leave, to rest a little and especially to buy a heavier hydraulic ram. That same evening, just after 10pm, four of the men return, and with the improved equipment, they manage to clear the gap to the locker room, so that after a night of hard work, the next morning, Easter Sunday the 4th of April, the burglars walk out around 6:45am with their plastic bins filled to the brim and drive away in their white van.

In these bins are the contents of seventy-three of the 999 lockers of Hatton Garden Safety Deposit Ltd: jewellery, gold and platinum bars, expensive watches, cash and other valuables with a total estimated value at the time of £14 million, of which only about a third has been recovered to date, partly hidden in tombs in a London cemetery.

The perfect crime, that is, the crime that is never solved or punished is a rare phenomenon. The Hatton Garden Heist, as it is known, was certainly not perfectly executed. The use of a private, strikingly white Mercedes for exploring the neighbourhood in advance and driving around later; purchasing the stronger hydraulic ram in one of their own names; and meeting together afterwards in a pub and bragging about the successful burglary, these were crucial flaws that caused the gang to be rolled up within six weeks, then sentenced to hefty prison terms.

From one of the seventy-three looted safe deposits emerged a remarkable gold ring, in the form of a belt closed with a buckle, in which, among other things, the year 1876 was engraved on the inside. In the London milieu of small and large thieves, receivers and jewellery dealers, the rumour soon started to circulate about this uncommon nineteenth-century ring, with the detail that a Russian text was engraved on the outside.

This story caught the attention of the well-known Dutch art detective Arthur Brand, nicknamed 'The Indiana Jones of the Art World,' who himself happens to be an enthusiastic admirer of Oscar Wilde. Born in 1969 and with an academic background in history, Brand has built an international reputation for recovering lost and stolen art treasures: paintings, mosaics, ornaments, rare books and even two bronze sculptures of horses that stood in front of the entrance to Adolf Hitler's Berlin chancellery. The art-historical sleuth remembered the theft of Oscar Wilde's ring at Oxford and realised that most likely this had to be the same jewel, and that an illiterate dealer had mistakenly identified the text as Russian instead of Greek.

Through the unfathomable ways and connections available to Brand, he was able to locate the man who had bought the ring in good faith, and who was shocked to hear that it was an Oscar Wilde-jewel stolen from Oxford University. On the 4th of December 2019, seventeen years after the original theft, the solemn return of the jewel took place in the library of Magdalen College, Oxford, where it can now be admired again in a—hopefully more secure—display case.

For a piece of gold jewellery from December 1876, these are unlikely adventures, ending up where the ring was originally presented as a gift, twice in fact: first by Oscar Wilde together with Reginald Harding and a few decades later by Willam Ward. Could such a spectacular quest also be undertaken in the case of Florence Balcombe's golden crucifix? Would the clever and well-connected Arthur Brand be able to force a breakthrough here too? The problem is that there does not exist a picture of our Victorian love cross, that it is not even known with certainty which name, names or initials are engraved in it. All this makes it extremely difficult to enlist even the most experienced and perspicacious art detective. Maybe I should first try and see for myself what other witnesses I can conjure, if not from reality, then at least from the imagination.

7

ENGAGED?

Little can be said with certainty about the inner emotional dimensions of Oscar Wilde's love life or about his sexual activities in his younger years. Based on the references to her in his letters, it appears that at least for a while he was madly in love with Florence Balcombe. In a questionnaire about his personal preferences that he completed in 1877 as a self-portrait, Wilde listed 'Florence' as one of his three favourite first names. Incidentally, when asked who, if not himself, he would rather be, his answer was: 'A Cardinal of the Catholic Church.'

The golden crucifix he gave to his Florence must have been quite a depletion of his budget as an undergraduate. Nothing is known of similar gifts in those same years to other girls. From her side, most of the correspondence between them has unfortunately not been preserved, but some of his love letters have survived and he has also repeatedly and enthusiastically written about her in letters to others. At the same time, you may wonder what this is worth, the appearance of being madly in love?

Oscar met Florence in Dublin, probably when he was staying for some time with his recently widowed mother in the family home on Merrion Square in the summer holidays of 1876. Florence's older sister, Philippa, he certainly liked too, but she was six years older, which at that stage of life is an almost unbridgeable difference. Oscar was twenty-one at the time, *Florrie*—as she was called in an intimate circle—had just turned eighteen on the 17th of July of that year. She was born in Cornwall and moved to Dublin with her parents as a two-year-old, when her father, an officer in the British Indian Army, had returned from Bombay. He had previously fought in the Crimean War, which has led some to believe that Florence was named after the famous nurse Florence Nightingale, so beloved by the British military. The family settled in the Clontarf district on the north side of Dublin, not far from the mouth of the Liffey, in a typical English semi-circular row of houses called Marino Crescent, with a beautiful unobstructed view at the front.

Florence Anne Lemon Balcombe was, to put it with a gender twist, a kind of female Dorian Gray: talented, a blank, still unwritten page, according to many an absolute beauty, and with her whole life still open in front of her. Oscar soon boasted to a college friend about his new girlfriend as 'exquisitely pretty' and having 'the most perfectly beautiful face.' Photos survive that confirm the truth of these statements. The Irish artist and writer George Du Maurier, writer Daphne's grandfather, called Florence Balcombe one of the three most beautiful women he had ever met, a rather masculine kind of compliment, and one that reflects nothing of the intelligence, the wit and the epistolary talent for which she was also known. Florrie's talents must have made it all the more frustrating that she, like her four sisters, did not receive any university education, due to lack of funds in the family.

In the spring of 1876, on the 19th of April, Oscar's father had passed away, and the financial prospects for his widow and their two sons were tenuous. Lady Wilde would not be able to continue living indefinitely in the large and expensive house in Dublin. That is why Oscar, in his praise of Florence, immediately mentions to the same college friend that she does not own a penny. For him as a scholarship student, that was a sore point. Nevertheless, they seem to have kept up their relationship for just over two years.

How to interpret the exact nature and extent of that relationship is another matter. In nineteenth-century Dublin it was well-understood that an infatuation, even if it was mutual, could not simply progress to an engagement without the consent of the parents, in particular the father of the girl. 'An engagement,' proclaims Lady Bracknell in *The Importance of Being Earnest* to the young man courting her daughter, 'should come on a young girl as a surprise, pleasant or unpleasant as the case may be. It is hardly a matter that she could be allowed to arrange for herself.' After all, an engagement was the announcement of a proposed marriage rather than the sealing of a crush. Things never got that far between Oscar and Florrie, no matter what *billets doux* and Easter cards were exchanged, and notwithstanding their joint church attendance and the engraved gold crucifix that Oscar gave her. Thus, this small gift lingered in the vacuum of symbolic and unripe intentions.

Moreover, where it came to possibly marriageable young women, Oscar did not limit his attention to Florence Balcombe. In those same years, his admiring eye also fell on Margaret

('Daisy') Bradley, daughter of the Master of University College Oxford, who would later gain some fame as a poet and novelist under her married name Margaret Louisa Woods. A decade after their romantic encounters, Oscar reviewed one of her novels in an editorial in *Woman's World*, where he called her book 'powerful', praised her 'fierce intensity' and compared her work to that of Dostoevsky and Maupassant.

There were other girls too, such as one Eva, with a well-meaning relative who recommended her to Oscar as 'promising' and indicated that a proposal on his part would certainly be taken seriously. And of course there were flirtatious exchanges and meetings during parties and receptions, which sometimes led to recriminations, as this passage from a letter from an indignant mother illustrates:

> Dear Oscar, I was very much pained the last time
> I was at your house when I went into the drawing
> room and saw Fidelia sitting upon your knee. Young
> as she is, she ought to have had (and so I told her)
> the instinctive delicacy that would have shrunk
> from it — but oh! Oscar, the thing was neither right,
> nor manly, nor gentlemanlike in you. You have
> disappointed me — nay, so low and vulgar was
> it, that I could not have believed anyone of refined
> mind capable of such a thing.

Given so many prohibitions and restrictions and thus the impossibility of occasionally doing something undetected that resembles what we consider nowadays to be normal intercourse between sexually mature people in their early twenties, it is not surprising that both Oscar Wilde and the many hundreds of other male students at Oxford sought an alternative way of experiencing some premarital sexual activity. Two paths presented themselves for this, apart from the always somewhat desolate practice of solo sex.

The first was visiting a prostitute. There were reportedly several of them in the university town, including one who was nicknamed *Old Jess*. This female sex worker, whose full name to my knowledge has not survived, has gained a certain notoriety in the extensive biographical literature about Oscar Wilde as the one who would have given him a syphilis infection. If Wilde did indeed have syphilis, a point of considerable disagreement. For some biographers a syphilis infection is the explanatory key to many events and phases in Wilde's life, up to and including his cause of death. This theory has been denied and disproved several times by authoritative medical specialists, yet it continues to crop up as a possibility, partly because it provides a neat explanation for various questions and episodes in Wilde's life. For example, a syphilis infection could explain why Wilde was reluctant to further his advances towards Florence Balcombe, since at the time doctors typically recommended complete sexual abstinence for at least two years after contracting the disease. The syphilis-theory would also explain why, as soon as the two-year waiting period was over, Wilde reacted so sharply to the reported marriage plans of Florence and Bram Stoker. Wilde would have liked to have heard this piece of news from Florence herself, he threw at her in a letter.

The second option for young men at Oxford to have some sexual satisfaction was the way of male love, ranging from more or less innocent romping up to full homosexual contact. In the innumerable versions of Oscar Wilde's life story, it is mainly the young Oxford student Lord Alfred Douglas who is assigned the role of his gay partner. He certainly played that role, but they did not meet until June 1891. Oscar was thirty-six at the time, Douglas, or *Bosie*, as he was called in small circles, was twenty. Although their relationship, lasting more than nine-years—cruelly interrupted by Wilde's two years in prison—certainly had a strong sexual charge, they soon preferred to get together with even younger boys, in hotel rooms, in *chambres séparées* of private restaurants, or in the boys' brothel of the pimp Alfred Taylor, who would eventually stand trial together with Wilde and receive the same punishment. But when Oscar Wilde was a student, the period we are presently talking about, Bosie, born in 1870, was still very far from being in the picture.

It is a question that cannot be answered with certainty, which boys or men in this earlier phase of his life led Oscar Wilde into homosexual love. The fact that such behaviour was only removed from the English Criminal Law in 1967, adds biographical relevance to this point, transcending simple curiosity.

The first man that Oscar Wilde had a sexual relationship with may have been the artist Frank Miles, two years his senior, whom he encountered in July 1876, the same summer he met Florence Balcombe. From late 1878 onward, Miles and Wilde shared a house in London for two and a half years, first in Salisbury Street, north of Hyde Park, later in Tite Street, south of that same park, in Chelsea. At both addresses they jointly gave so-called 'beauty parties', house parties for what we would nowadays call socialites. This joint *ménage* came to a sudden end when Frank Miles' father, out of disgust with Wilde's published poems, forbade his son to continue the cohabitation, threatening to withdraw his allowance. Miles chose the money, and Wilde stormed indignantly out of the house.

Was Oscar Wilde already a sexually active gay man at the time he was courting Florence Balcombe? Was that perhaps the reason, rather than a syphilis infection, that he put so little energy into developing their relationship? A definitive answer to that question cannot be given. Wilde was a young poet, with great linguistic ability and enormous promise as an academic. At the same time, he was torn between uncertainty and self-importance, and like so many of his contemporaries, he felt trapped in the social restrictions of Victorian England. At one point during this period, apparently in desperation, he turned to the Catholic Church, although at the last moment he recoiled from a final conversion. Instead of going himself, he sent a large bunch of lilies to the Brompton Oratory, the London Catholic church that had declared itself willing to receive him.

Despite his meagre finances, Wilde was an optimist, with a not-too-realistic view of what his future would look like. In a memoir of their student days, his friend and contemporary at Oxford, the very Roman Catholic David Hunter-Blair, recollected that Wilde, when asked about his ambition in life, once answered: 'God knows, I won't be a dried-up Oxford don, anyhow. I'll be a poet, a writer, a dramatist. Somehow or other I'll be famous, and if not famous, I'll be notorious.' That does not sound like a vision of the future in which there would be much room for marriage or fatherhood.

For many years, Wilde kept in touch with Florence's older sister, Philippa. During his editorship of *Woman's World*, a high-quality fashion and art magazine aimed at a female readership, they even corresponded about an article Philippa might contribute. The first sentence of Wilde's letter to her (presumably from 1888) strongly suggests how much he cherished the fond memories of their former friendship: 'My dear Phil, I was delighted to see your handwriting again; it was like a touch of old days.' Even if you discount some of Wilde's usual exaggeration, this letter still breathes the air of a somewhat infatuated friendship, a genuine affinity, behind which there is perhaps more than just regret about his failed love for her younger sister.

A few years before this letter, Wilde visited the Balcombes again in Dublin, on Tuesday the 6th of January, 1885. Perhaps the whole family was at home together for the Christmas holidays, but whether Florrie was also present that evening cannot be ascertained. In the afternoon Wilde gave a lecture, as part of a tour that took him for months throughout England, Ireland and Scotland. Although he had gained the necessary experience as a speaker during his extensive American lecture tour, it remained an exhausting existence, about which he complains to Philippa in the letter announcing his visit. That evening in the beautiful house on Marino Crescent, with the view of the park and Dublin Bay in the distance, must have given Wilde all the pleasure of being reunited with people and with a house he still held dear. His married life with Constance Lloyd, who was pregnant with their first child at the time, had already lost its greatest appeal for him, despite their beautiful home in the sought-after Chelsea district that they had decorated and furnished entirely to their own taste.

On that January day in 1885, in the house of his former girlfriend and her dear older sister, the past may have seemed more attractive to him than the present. Will he have mentioned the little golden crucifix again that night, or would he have gotten the jewel back from Florence long before? Or had he forgotten the whole thing by now? The latter seems unlikely for a hypersensitive young poet. It was one of the few tangible reminders of what he had called in a letter to Florence 'two sweet years—the sweetest of all the years of my youth.'

8

MARRIED

The sudden marriage between the now twenty-year-old Florence Balcombe and thirty-one-year-old Bram—full name Abraham—Stoker has all the characteristics of an elopement, marriage as a joint escape. There was no time for a normal period of engagement, nor did they go on a honeymoon. The reasons for all this haste were manifold. To begin with, Florence as a 'Dublin beauty' may have had her much-praised looks as well as her talents, but Lieutenant Colonel James Balcombe unfortunately did not have the money to marry off his five daughters in an appropriate way. Bram Stoker's proposal was therefore a welcome opportunity, especially after the two years Florence had spent as the half-girlfriend of Oscar Wilde, studying at far-away Oxford. Wilde certainly had a brilliant mind, but he was also maladjusted and unconventional, with his Catholic leanings and the many weeks he sometimes let go by without a word. And he didn't have any money either, not even after his father's recent passing.

Bram Stoker was a lot more believable as a husband-to-be, not least because his parents were firmly Church of Ireland and attended services in the parish church of the same

Clontarf district on the north side of Dublin where the Balcombe family lived. After an early childhood in which he had been plagued by a crippling and mysterious disease, Stoker had grown up healthy and sound as the third of seven children and had studied at Trinity College, where he had even excelled in the field of athletics and rugby. As a student, he had begun writing magazine articles and theatre criticism for the local press. There was no money to be made from this—for that, at the insistence of his father Stoker had taken up a job as clerk at the magistrates' courts in Dublin Castle—but it yielded him his first contacts in the world of the theatre, where he was eager to find himself a real job. Following a very positive review of a *Hamlet* performance by Henry Irving, Stoker met the great actor in 1876, and they immediately formed a bond with each other.

Thus in 1878, when Irving took over the Lyceum Theatre in London's West End, where he had played his *Hamlet* no less than two hundred times, he offered Bram the position of business manager, which the latter immediately accepted. Instead of his mind-numbing and poorly paid clerk job in Dublin, Stoker could now build a new life together with Florence in London, the theatre capital of the British Isles.

The exact nature of the bond between Irving and Stoker has been the subject of much speculation over the years, but it had a momentous impact. In his *Personal Reminiscences of Henry Irving* (1906) Stoker would write about their first encounter: 'Soul had looked into soul. From that hour began a friendship as profound, as close, as lasting as can be between two men.' On that same occasion Irving presented him with an autographed portrait photo with the handwritten text 'My dear friend Stoker. God bless

Bram Stoker some years into his marriage to Florence Balcombe

you! God bless you!!'. Their friendship lasted twenty-seven years and would only be ended by Irving's death.

It is doubtful whether Stoker's emotional state, as it comes across in this relationship with his employer, was such a promising starting point for his upcoming married life with Florence Balcombe, but the job as manager of the successful Lyceum Theatre provided at least the necessary financial basis for their new existence.

At the time of his removal together with Florence to London thirty-one-year-old Stoker, in addition to a few short stories, numerous theatre reviews and journalistic articles, had written a short novel, *The Primrose Path* (1875). That book is the story of newlywed carpenter Jerry O'Sullivan who moves to London from Dublin, along with his wife Katey and their three young children. Instead of settling down firmly in the solid job he has found at the theatre, he tragically perishes in the capital, mainly from alcohol abuse, seduced by a Mephistophelian figure. In the end, he gruesomely kills his wife with a blow of his hammer against her temple, after which he cuts his own throat with his chisel and dies next to her. It is a rather drab and moralistic story, but it certainly underscores how Stoker's mind was set years ago on the idea of working in the theatre in London.

The young couple settled on the top floor of a mixed-use apartment and office building on Southampton Street, just a few hundred yards away from the Lyceum Theatre, and their lives in the years that followed would be entirely dominated by his work. To a certain extent, of course, this was—and is—in the nature of the theatre. As the Lyceum's business manager, Bram was rarely home before midnight, after he had collected and administered the evening's receipts. Not to mention Irving's regular tours in England, Europe and the United States, accompanied by Stoker, for weeks or even months on end. And when he was at home, Stoker worked frantically in his study on new novels and stories, eager to acquire a public profile as a writer, in addition to his business position behind the scenes of the Lyceum.

A few years into his married life, Stoker published, presumably at his own expense, seven rather spooky fairy tales, in a beautifully produced volume with elaborate illustrations entitled *Under the Sunset*. This was followed by several other attempts to impress the literary world with narrative prose: the novel *The Snake's Pass*, a chapter in a collectively undertaken feuilleton novel (*The Fate of Fenella*), followed shortly afterwards by the novels *The Watter's Mou'* and *The Shoulder of Shasta*. All completely forgotten books, on which the author nevertheless laboured late at night and early in the morning, at the expense of his sleep, his marriage and his family life.

Around 1881, the Stokers moved to the address 26 Cheyne Walk in the Chelsea district favoured among artists and intellectuals, not far from the north bank of the river Thames. In the meantime, in 1879, they had had a son, who was baptised Irving Noel Thornley Stoker. In the light of his father's frequent and prolonged absences, the boy was raised exclusively by his mother, and as soon as he had something to say about it himself, he would drop his first name 'Irving' in favour of his second baptismal name (Noel), out of resentment towards the dominant actor who had taken such a heavy toll on his father's life. In a 1959 letter to Stoker's first biographer Harry Ludlam, but not revealed until 2016 by the subsequent biographer David J. Skal, Noel Stoker mentioned an argument between his parents, with his mother reproaching her husband that he would probably be saddened more by the death of Henry Irving than that of his own son. To this Bram Stoker reportedly responded angrily that a child can be replaced, but not Henry Irving.

None of which adds up to a very flourishing picture of the Stoker marriage. And yet, there must also have been positive, even festive moments: first nights, receptions and interesting encounters in the artistic, literary and theatrical world. Over the years, prominent artists produced portraits of Florence, just as her admirer Oscar Wilde had done in their younger years in Dublin. Bram and Florence even attended receptions at the home of Wilde, who also lived in Chelsea with his wife Constance and their two young sons. Given the fact that Wilde was gradually making a name for himself in the theatre, the two couples inevitably ran into each other at first nights and on other occasions. Several brief letters from Oscar to Bram have been preserved, mainly requests for theatre seats, and to Florence he sent inscribed copies of new books he published, such as his volume of fairy tales *The Happy Prince* in 1888, and in 1893 a copy of his Biblical drama *Salomé*.

During all this time, where was the crucifix that Oscar had given to Florence on Christmas Day in 1876, when they both probably still assumed that their lives would forever be linked? Had Florence kept the little golden cross and, if so, did she ever take it out, in a mood of slight melancholy for her former infatuation and the expectations she had cherished of married life? Or had she returned the cross to Wilde, something he had expressly requested by letter, saying that the thing would no longer be of any value to her and that it was a precious souvenir to him. And if Florence still had the crucifix, would her husband Bram ever have seen this piece of jewellery? Around her neck? And if so, did he know the story behind it?

A horrifying event may have cast a permanent stain on the Stokers' house in Chelsea, at least in the eyes of the sensitive Florence. In the night of the 14th of September, 1882, on his way home on a ferry boat after a performance of *Romeo and Juliet* at the Lyceum, Bram rescued a suicide from the waters of the Thames. Together with a group of passengers, he brought the dripping body of the drowned man into their home, placed it on the dining table in the living room, after which a doctor pronounced the man dead. One can imagine any lady of a house, having been woken up in the middle of the night, being in shock upon witnessing such a scene in her own dining-room. In any event, three years later the Stokers moved to a smaller and less attractive house in Chelsea, on 17 St. Leonard's Terrace.

It was at this address that in March 1890 Bram Stoker had a curious dream about a young man who goes out and sees a number of girls, one of whom tries to kiss him, not on the mouth but on his neck, after which an old Count intervenes, exclaiming angrily: 'This man belongs to me, I want him.' As an expression of the subconscious of a young, hard-working family man, it was rather disturbing, but as a starting point for writing a horror novel, it turned out to be quite fertile.

9

KISS

At what age does a person have a fully developed self? In the domain of psychology, or philosophy if you will, this is perhaps a non-issue, because everyone continues to develop throughout their life and within that development there is not one stage in which the self is more itself than before or after. Every stage is, in a sense, an intermediate stage, until one day life is over. Yet from a biographical perspective many famous lives are encapsulated at a stage that becomes indelible: the grey-haired scientific genius that was Albert Einstein, the eloquent black civil rights activist Martin Luther King, the haughty and other-worldly pre-revolutionary Queen Marie-Antoinette. All famous personalities have such a single public image based on their greatest recognisability, one image in which their individual character seems to be developed to the full. That is why it is so strange to suddenly see a childhood portrait of someone who gained great fame later in life or—vice versa—to see a photo of a well-known Hollywood actor or actress at a very old age. In our imagination, the former were never young and the latter will never grow old.

When looking at the phenomenon of Oscar Wilde, one must consider two particularities. The first is that he lived to be only forty-six years old. His adult life, from his graduation at Oxford and his move to London in late 1878, up to his demise in Paris, lasted no more than twenty-two years, and that includes the two years he spent in prison, when his life was put on hold. Wilde's imprisonment—and this is the second particularity—forms the great watershed of his life, resulting in not one, but two emblematic images to choose from: either the startling and scandalous success story before his conviction in 1895, or the tragic and broken martyrdom after his release in 1897. These two contrasting images form a perfect Wildean paradox, since both concern the same person.

Let us turn to that initial stage up to 1895, when Wilde emerged as a rising star on the literary-journalistic and cultural firmament of London. Although his Irish origin made him an outsider in the established circles of London society, Wilde soon acquired a conspicuous, albeit controversial position with daring, witty and suggestive writings: journalistic articles, art criticism, essays, literary and dramatic reviews, poems, short stories and the novel *The Picture of Dorian Gray*. The crowning achievement of this period were the four satirical plays, performed with great success in the theatres of the London West End between 1892 and 1895. Wilde's way of dressing, manner of speaking and his astounding social manners complemented this creative production. The grand total of this performance meant that no one in late-nineteenth-century London could avoid forming an opinion about the personality of Oscar Wilde. It is a compelling image, one that Wilde assiduously cultivated, and whose origins can be traced to the full year—from the 2nd of

January to the 27th of December, 1882—that Wilde travelled for an extensive lecture tour in the US and in Canada.

This remarkable tour was conceived as a PR-stunt by the English theatre impresario and hotel entrepreneur Richard D'Oyly Carte. Originally working as a musician and conductor, he soon chose the business side of the entertainment world. He was the one who brought librettist William Gilbert and composer Arthur Sullivan together and even had an entire opera theatre built in London (with later a Grand Hotel next to it), where a long series of immensely successful comic operas by this duo were staged. One of those operas was *Patience; or, Bunthorne's Bride,* a satire on the so-called 'aesthetes', a movement of artists and poets that many people saw as offensive and pretentious, and of which Oscar Wilde publicly presented himself as an advocate.

After a successful series of try-outs at the small London Opera Comique, the play premiered at the large Savoy Theatre on the 10th of October 1881. Hundreds of performances in a theatre with 1,292 seats, sold-out night after night, a success that D'Oyly Carte next attempted to monetise in America. The first performances in New York were promising enough, but there was no time to lose, because due to the lack of international copyright treaties, pirates were always lurking in the US to bring successful English productions to the theatre without paying any royalties.

This gave rise to the idea of sending Oscar Wilde to America, as the self-proclaimed leader of the English aesthetes, by way of mascot for this theatre production. His frequent appearance in the satirical weekly magazine *Punch,* where in cartoons he was ridiculed for his aesthetic attire, his personal cult of beauty and his affected way of speaking, showed that he decidedly had publicity potential. According to the original plan there would be a few dozen lectures, spread over a couple of weeks, but once on the spot, the stunt turned out to work so well, and was so agreeable to Wilde himself, that eventually he would travel around the North American continent for a full year and give about one hundred and fifty lectures in more than one hundred cities in the US and Canada.

As a reference to the extremely sensitive *Patience*-protagonist Bunthorne, Wilde, often dressed in aesthetically over-refined clothes, addressed the paying public about beauty in everyday life, about the value of craftsmanship, about the aesthetic movement in England that he presented as a new Renaissance, about home furnishings and interior art and thus about the importance of materials, colours and the right combinations thereof. He had also prepared a lecture on Irish poetry and about the English poets of the nineteenth century. In all these lectures he relied heavily on the ideas of established English writers, poets and thinkers such as William Morris, Walter Pater, Dante Gabriel Rossetti, John Ruskin and Algernon Charles Swinburne, but far away from home he could unconcernedly make their ideas his own and embellish them.

It can be guessed that for a typical American audience in 1882, especially in venues outside the big cities on the East Coast, this was all very high-flown and although Wilde, entitled to a third of all net proceeds, earned the nice sum of $5,605.31 at the end of the year (about $175,000 in 2025), the reactions of the press and public were not always positive. But that did not really matter. He was often and extensively written about, and this lecturing year did yield him a lot, not just in financial terms. Instead of Wilde promoting the performances, in the end it was rather the other way around:

the whole PR-circus made him famous, both in the US and in England, where his transatlantic exploits were widely reported, discussed, and sometimes ridiculed. These American experiences contributed in no small way to the evolution of the twenty-seven-year-old Irish journalist and aspiring poet into the Oscar Wilde we still know today.

To begin with, in America Wilde learned to obey and apply the laws of modern publicity, especially their visual component. Soon after arriving in New York, he was photographed in his Union Square studio by the American portrait photographer of the day, Napoleon Sarony, who for commercial uses made more than twenty different portraits of him. Furthermore, the young Wilde learned how to give quick and easily quotable answers during interviews, even when asked nonsensical or irrelevant questions. During his stay he gave at least ninety-eight interviews, which also sharpened his wit and his talent for epigram. While at first he lectured his audiences rather laboriously, after a few months he had a better understanding of how to modulate his voice, how to vary his presentation, how to forge a bond with the people in the hall and how an audience wants to be amused, but not too emphatically taught.

This extensive tour in America also made him thoroughly familiar with being on the road for a long time and dining out in restaurants almost daily, something he would continue to cultivate as a habit after returning to England and also later on the European continent. In fact, except for the first two years of his marriage, Wilde actually never again led a regular domestic life and felt most at home in hotels and restaurants. He also learned how to deal with fans and fan mail during his tour, and how to play the role of guest of honour at a party or a dinner. Furthermore, his assignment to promote *Patience* inspired him to adopt an even more expressive dressing-style than he was already used to. During his tour he was offered the services of a black servant named William Traquair, whose permanent availability must have further heightened the young poet's sense of status. And finally, 1882 was the year in which he was able to spend (other people's) money unconcernedly for the first time in his life: in hotels and restaurants, in shops and in train stations, on tips and gifts. For most culinary and alcoholic indulgences he probably never even saw a bill, thus inculcating a lifelong habit of ignoring the cost of an extravagant lifestyle as much as possible.

Apart from these useful experiences and his encounters with politicians, with actors and especially actresses, and with some of the best-known American writers of the day, there was in particular one meeting during his American year that gave Oscar Wilde a poetic, spiritual and even existential experience for the rest of his life, and that was his visit in January 1882 to the then almost legendary American poet Walt Whitman in Camden, New Jersey.

Wilde owed this meeting, just a few weeks after his arrival on the *SS Arizona* in the port of New York, to the mediation of Joseph M. Stoddart, who as a publisher was regularly in touch with Whitman. Stoddart, publisher of almanacs, encyclopaedias and of the successful *Lippincott's Monthly Magazine*, was indirectly involved in Wilde's promotional tour, as he had acquired the American publishing rights to *Patience* and all of Gilbert and Sullivan's other operas. The more attention Wilde's presence in the US would attract, the better. A visit from Wilde to Whitman fitted that ambition perfectly.

Stoddart's plan turned out to be an immediate hit. OSCAR, THE AESTHETE. HIS FAST-APPROACHING VISIT TO PHILADELPHIA,

Walt Whitman in 1882, the year Oscar Wilde
visited him in Camden, NJ

one newspaper headlined, while another proclaimed: PHIL-
ADELPHIA HONORED BY PROLONGED VISITS FROM THE POET. In
an interview with the *Philadelphia Press*, in which Wilde was
asked what American poet he admired most, he thoughtfully
paved the way for his desired meeting: 'I think that Walt
Whitman and Emerson have given the world more than anyone else. I do so hope to meet Mr Whitman.'

That outstretched hand was much appreciated by the
poet of *Leaves of Grass*, the revolutionary collection originally
published in 1855, and via Stoddart he wrote a note with an
invitation for the two gentlemen to come over. And so, on

the 18th of January 1882, the day after a still somewhat stiff lecture before an audience of fifteen hundred paying visitors in Philadelphia's *Horticultural Hall*, Oscar Wilde, along with Stoddart, crossed the Delaware river by ferry to the industrial city of Camden, New Jersey. There, the older Whitman, partially paralysed after a stroke, lived in an upstairs room in the home of one of his brothers and the latter's wife on 431 Stevens Street (a wooden house unfortunately burned to the ground in 1994). The visit lasted a good two hours and publisher Stoddart had the rare tact to go for a walk, so that the two poets, provided first with a milk punch and then elderberry wine, could retire together quietly to Whitman's own room on the third floor.

At first glance, it seems like an unlikely combination: the sixty-two-year-old bearded poet of uninhibited free verse, which grew almost organically in all directions in successive editions of *Leaves of Grass*, communing with the twenty-seven-year-old, academically trained apostle of aestheticism, whose poems tried to excel above all in fidelity to form, metre and rhyme. But on looking closer, there are certain parallels that must have established an immediate bond between the two.

Both poets were outsiders to the social and literary establishment of their country. Whitman was—in his own words—'an old rough', with a chequered career behind him, a jack-of-all-trades and master of none, especially when compared to the kind of neat trinomial gentlemen like William Cullen Bryant and Henry Wadsworth Longfellow who had hitherto been the figureheads of American poetry. For his part, the cheeky young Irish poet and journalist Wilde was himself an outsider trying to get in, a pretentious upstart in the eyes of many. Both poets were accused early on of endangering morals with the excess of sexual charge in their work and the maladjustment in their social behaviour. There was a persistent atmosphere of doubt, depravity and immorality about them. Both their earliest published poetry was mocked, even in the form of parodies that appeared of their work. To this they both responded with a kind of theatrical energy and a huge work drive, Whitman as the exuberant opera lover he was, and Wilde as someone who regarded the whole of London social life as one big theatre-play. Based on their experience as journalists and reviewers, both had a good understanding of the best way to promote their own work, and because they both saw poetry as their philosophy of life, there was no difference between promoting their work and promoting their personality.

In an interview he gave the next day to the *Philadelphia Press* Whitman spoke enthusiastically about their meeting. 'We had a very happy time together' he declared, and added, while reportedly stroking his silvery beard, 'He seemed to me like a great big, splendid boy.' Wilde, for his part, later bragged to an English friend: 'I have the kiss of Walt Whitman still on my lips.'

That last quote is a reminder that Walt Whitman's sexuality is possibly even more difficult to capture in one term than Oscar Wilde's. Do Whitman's poems sing of fraternisation, combined with an informal and easy physicality? Or was Whitman indeed gay, but at a time when it was better to hide that truth? Or was he bisexual, considering his many physical and sexual references to women?

The point is that these kinds of sexual-identitarian terms were not at all common in the 1880s and that the underlying phenomena were also much less clearly defined than they are today. Perhaps one should not classify Whitman's free handling of the physical in the separate modern-day boxes of sexual nomenclature at all, just as his poems do not fit into the poetic form of sonnets and quatrains and his verses do not obey the laws of the iambic pentameter or the alexandrine.

Walt Whitman's appeal to many young people lay precisely in the ideal image of his transcendental, natural and philosophical pansexuality. Whitman's poetic gospel of camaraderie thus constituted a liberation from the obligatory dichotomy between the heterosexual and the homosexual, the constrained choice between the male and the female, on which basis homosexuality would soon be labelled with the Freudian term 'inversion'. In him was a kind of generosity with which he erased, both in his work and in his way of life, the boundary between his own body and that of others.

In this atmosphere, it seems entirely fitting, although in 1882 it was of course highly unusual, that the two poets would have kissed each other on the mouth. It was a fitting conclusion of what was in many ways a special encounter, and for Wilde this kiss remained an unforgettable symbolic seal on his personality that he was trying to perfect as a work of art. As an invisible jewel, he would continue to carry this symbolic kiss with him through all the highs and lows of his later life. Or as Whitman himself wrote in one of his poems: 'More shining than the Cross, more than the Crown, / The height to be superb humanity.'

And Florence Balcombe, what in her later life was the significance of the kisses she had received from Oscar Wilde? And of the golden jewel that she had worn around her neck, at least for a while, as a symbol of their love? Did she ever write something about it in her later life, reminisced about what Oscar had called their 'two sweet years'? Were her memories as sweet as his, as the years went by? Unfortunately, in the absence of obvious sources, there are no easy ways to find answers to these questions across the line between life and death. The best I can think of is to call up all possible witnesses who could directly or indirectly contribute something of value to our search.

How, for example, would Florence's older sister Philippa have looked back on her memories of the young Oscar Wilde? In all the biographical literature about the writer, her silhouette is even more indistinct than that of Florence, but does not that give me exactly the necessary room to imagine how she had kept Oscar in her mind, and perhaps also a little in her heart?

10

SISTER

Philippa Knott slowly lowers the newspaper. She feels
the blood flowing in her arms. As soon as the rustling
of the paper has stopped, she remains motionless. From
her favourite chair in the bay window of the sitting
room, she looks down the street, in the direction of St.
Stephen's Green. The fog that hung in the street this
morning has lifted and now you can see all the way to
the first trees of the park. It is not really cold outside,
and taking advantage of the dry weather she took a
walk with a friend earlier this Thursday. It was bare
in the park among the leafless trees and there weren't
many other walkers, but the fresh air was lovely. Other
people long for spring at the beginning of winter, but
not Philippa, who loves the quiet, peaceful cold in the
city. This always gives her additional energy.

With a deep sigh, she holds up the paper again
and looks at the short article on page 2 of the Dublin
Evening Mail. Behind her eyes, she feels that she could
cry. She is not going to, though, because that would
be ridiculous and, besides, it has all been far too long.

*But the news grips her, because isn't that the saddest
thing, that everything that passes can suddenly seem
so utterly meaningless? And that in the end nothing,
nothing at all, remains?*

*In that respect, the past few years have been harsh
anyway. Philippa looks out the window again; her gaze
is blurred, and in her mind, she sees very different
figures than the people who occasionally pass by the
house. First Father had gone, then Mother and then
her eldest brother. Philippa realises that she hasn't
been to Mount Jerome Cemetery for too long, not even
last month, on the 18th of October, the anniversary of
her brother's death. In this way, of course, she herself
contributes to the senselessness she complains about,
and she feels guilty about neglecting her duty towards
her loved ones.*

*She focuses on the newspaper again. The article in
the* Dublin Evening Mail *is based on a report from the
Paris correspondent. It says that in a hotel in the Paris
Latin Quarter, the formerly well-known playwright
and literary author Oscar Wilde is dying. Mention is
being made of meningitis and the opinion of the doctors treating him that there is no chance of recovery.*

*With that reference to his past fame, it sounds
all the more like someone from a completely different
era is dying. And perhaps that is true, Philippa thinks,
although the article mentions the writer being forty-six
years old. She herself is now fifty-two, wife and mother
of two wonderful children. Not for the first time, she
feels terrified at the thought that her own life could suddenly be over. That is the weird thing about death: once*

you have seriously encountered the finality of life a few times, the vulnerability of everything never leaves you again, like a threat that remains close by. How could one ever protect one's children from this?

Philippa feels that sitting here alone she should not start reminiscing now. This evening they will have guests, for which everything still has to be prepared. Nevertheless, her thoughts involuntarily go back to the time when Florence and she had long conversations about the promising student who wrote such flowery poems. Florrie was seventeen or eighteen and she herself was twenty-seven, twenty-eight. That ten-year difference in age with her younger sister accompanies them as a constant distance throughout their lives. For a while, they talked about little else than the young poet who fascinated them both. Living in Oxford as a student, he occasionally stayed at his parents' house in Dublin.

Philippa puts the newspaper aside, leans her head back and closes her eyes for a moment, while in the quiet house on York Street on this the 29th of November of the year 1900, the clock in the front room gently ticks. The house is in complete tranquillity, now that Billie and Eleanor are staying with one of Philippa's other sisters. And their housekeeper Mary is running errands with the new kitchen help. Upstairs in his study, her husband John is working on a new article. Work, work, work, is that the best thing a man can think of, when for once he is home a little earlier in the afternoon?

Which of them met Oscar first, Philippa would not be able to say anymore, but it was clear they both immediately found him attractive and interesting. It was just before or just after Florrie's eighteenth birthday, probably after, when her sister began to be invited into various family homes in Dublin. Maybe it was at Oscar's parents that their decisive meeting took place, in the large corner house on Merrion Square.

Peculiar people, both of them. Oscar's mother was tall in stature, always wearing extravagant dresses and with an exaggerated way of speaking, barely distinguishing between reciting poems and stating arguments. She did not converse like other hostesses, but talked as if she were addressing an entire theatre. Both her poetry and her ordinary conversation were distinctly political in character, and her presence as a hostess always made a particularly dramatic impression.

And then Oscar's father, a head shorter than his wife, an elusive scholar, who sometimes presented himself as an archaeologist, sometimes as a medical man, and always as a narrator of the most abstruse histories and mythological stories. He had travelled extensively, from which he had acquired a great deal of exotic knowledge, and his historical and archaeological interest in Ireland was also a rich source for his conversation.

Sometimes Philippa felt that her own husband's profile as a doctor and an erudite and versatile scholar had something in common with Sir William. The subjects of all those articles and pamphlets that John worked on year after year, where did he get it from? Disease histories of Napoleon and of Lord Byron were fair enough for a physician with a historical interest, but why spend time on writing about spontaneous combustion, phrenology, female circumcision?

Like Oscar's father, John was a bit of an eccentric and bookish scholar, but at the same time he was very caring and when he made time for Billie and Eleanor, he was a devoted and loving father, and fortunately his appearance had little in common with Sir William's. Philippa used to think it was something of a punishment to have to shake hands with Oscar's father as a greeting or farewell when she was a guest at one of their at homes. There was always a faint atmosphere around him of filth. Bah.

The gossip that in his novel Dracula *Bram had based the character of the vampire-fighting Professor Van Helsing on John was completely unfounded, Bram had reassured her. Like Florrie, she found that whole book a rather distasteful and repulsive affair. Why would one want to engage in that kind of bizarre fantasy? John was perhaps a trifle dull, but the world of his thoughts was a lot healthier than Bram's.*

As a girl, Florence had been an absolute beauty, Philippa had to admit. In the past, there had sometimes been some rivalry between the five Balcombe sisters towards potential marriage candidates. But that was long ago and now that Philippa had passed fifty, the age difference with Florence weighed less and less. At the time, it made sense that Oscar, who must then have been twenty-two or twenty-three, fell in love with Florrie. Philippa herself also felt something special for him and she was convinced that this affinity was mutual,

*but it had always been clear to both of them that this
involved more friendly sentiments than feelings of love.
Perhaps if the age difference had been smaller? Nonsense,
Philippa had never begrudged her sister his admiration
for her during those years, and indeed from others.*

*Nevertheless, Philippa felt that between Oscar
and herself, something of their former confidentiality
had always remained. Years later, after a lecture
in his hometown, he had visited her again. He had
not been married long and had a whole year of lecturing in America and Canada behind him. Perhaps
that accounted for his new-found self-assurance. But
Philippa had also seen fatigue and unspoken doubts
and problems in his face. With John present, the conversation had not been so personal that she could have
said or asked anything about it.*

*They had hardly spoken about Florrie that evening,
but she must have been in his thoughts all the same.
From the beginning, Oscar had completely doted on
her. He had made a portrait drawing of her, in one of
her most beautiful dresses. Honestly, as a portrait it
did not seem such a success, although it was definitely
a beautifully drawn girl's face and at least it proved
that he loved her. And that he could draw quite nicely.
Later, he had also given her a landscape in watercolour,
painted around where his parents had a country house.
With the best will in the world, you could not tell the
water from the trees or the trees from the hills, so
soupy were the colours. But he signed it gracefully and
underneath his signature he had written something
sweet for Florrie, which was of course all that counted.*

*Father had been less enthusiastic about all these
rapprochements and demonstrations of love, and more
than once he had been about to ask young Wilde by
letter for clarification of his intentions. Fortunately,
Philippa was able to talk him out of this. In her mind's
eye, she could still see the draft of a letter lying on the
desk in his study, while he gave a long monologue to
explain his point of view. Father had just then been
promoted to lieutenant colonel. He had always been
extremely strict in his upbringing, when it comes to
rules of conduct in social life. At this height of his military career, he seemed morally more demanding than
ever. He simply found Oscar too cheeky and also too
loose in his dealings with Florence. With five daughters,
Father believed that in this respect he could not afford
any leniency. What also bothered him in no small
measure were Oscar's Roman sympathies. Even during
visits to their home, he often talked about the beauty
of cathedrals, Italian altarpieces and the special appeal
of the Catholic Mass. Did he not realise that the Balcombe family was one hundred percent Church of
Ireland, or did he do this on purpose to make himself
interesting, or to provoke a little?*

*In any case, Florrie was deeply impressed at the
time by what he said and did, and their companionship
perhaps contributed to her taking an interest in the
Roman faith. In her idea, something she did not dare
to confess to Father, it was a spiritual current that rose
above the seriousness and the grind and the tediousness
of Protestantism. Philippa would not be surprised if her
sister would go over to the church of Rome, especially*

now that Father was no longer there to stop her. In that case, her former relationship with Oscar would in the end still produce an effect, all those years later. How long ago was it? More than twenty years!

In retrospect, Father's worries were unnecessary. For a year or two they did exchange letters and cards, but a real engagement or even serious plans for it had never been in the air, although Oscar reacted with great disappointment when at the age of twenty Florence accepted Bram's proposal. Shortly after that marriage announcement, Philippa and Oscar had met again at her parents' house, on a day when Florrie was not at home. All of a sudden, not much was left of the invincible charmer, Philippa recalled. He was pouting a little about his thwarted infatuation, forgetting that he himself had sometimes neglected it for weeks on end. The year before he had travelled to Italy and Greece for more than a month with his former professor at Trinity plus a few other students, and all this time he had not paid any attention to Florrie, although she had even written to him in Athens.

As he sat across from her, in the same room on Marino Crescent where he had visited them so many times, Philippa had wanted to laugh at him a little, when he talked in such a dramatic way about the loss of his marriage chances. With broad hand gestures, with which he also occasionally wiped the strands of straight hair from his face, he was almost acting like a prince on stage, pining for some distant beloved. Philippa had told him candidly what she thought. That was the advantage of being a few years older.

When they said goodbye, he mentioned he would
like a present to be returned to him, that he had given
to Florrie two years before, on the day they had gone
to Christmas service together: a small golden crucifix. Not that it was such a valuable thing, he insisted,
but it seemed more fitting for him to take possession
of it again. After all, she would not wear it anymore.
Philippa remembered how he had looked at her pen-
etratingly and repeated that for him it represented a
special memory of the past two years. Philippa simply said that she would convey his request. In such
emotional negotiations, she preferred not to interfere.
Now, so many years later, she doesn't know where this
small piece of jewellery ended up.

She is curious how Florrie will respond to Oscar's
imminent passing in Paris. In about three weeks, over
Christmas, they will definitely see each other, perhaps
at Florrie's home in London or else here with the rest
of the family in Dublin. And Oscar, how long will he
have to wait for redemption? Under the circumstances,
the report about his deathbed is not a subject to raise
before by letter.

Florrie has been married to Bram for more than
twenty years, and if there is a shadow of her past
hanging over that marriage, it is not for Philippa to
bring up the subject. She herself knows all too well that
an earlier love story remains a permanent presence
in the background of a later marriage. So it is with
her own John, whom Philippa married two years after
the tragic death of his first wife. Sometimes she feels
that John's relentless work discipline also serves as

an escape from this memory. At the same time, she is convinced that they are both unconditionally fond of each other and firmly connected. Their two energetic and intelligent children are the best proof of this.

How other shadows may have fallen over Florrie's marriage to Bram, is hard to say even for an older sister. Spontaneous, energetic, vivid infatuation is perhaps by definition a short-lived moment in one's younger life, and not something that two people can hold up to each other for years. Florrie and Bram seem satisfied with their life together and with their grown son, who by now is almost twenty-one himself and studying at Oxford. But how many times in recent years has Philippa seen her sister truly elated and happy? Her letters are usually quite matter of fact in tone, and they make it clear that Bram travels a lot, and that Florrie is often left to her own devices. A few years ago, when she came to stay together with Irving for a week in the summer, she had proudly shown a gold ring that Bram had given her, with a large blood-red garnet in it. That had been one of those rare moments, in which Florrie's delighted look of being in love had shown again.

Philippa starts from her musings and looks at the clock. At the same time, she hears the kitchen door, and knows that Mary has returned. As she picks up the newspaper from the floor and puts it folded on a side table, she also hears John coming down the stairs. A moment later, her husband enters the room with a broad smile, which Philippa knows indicates his satisfaction that he has finished his article in time for their visitors. She rises from her chair, happy that after her silent musing in response to the nasty newspaper article, the house around her comes back to life. She feels like she's been somewhere far away. She walks up to John on a whim and hugs him, to which he responds with restrained surprise. 'My dear, to what do I owe this sudden display of affection?'

'Just because,' says Philippa with something of a smile on her face, 'you are my husband and I am your wife,' and without revealing her thoughts she walks out of the room toward the voices coming at her from the kitchen.

11

EVENING

Publishers generally do not have a very good reputation in literary history. At worst, they are greedy, opportunistic, and rather ill-mannered types, who greatly exaggerate the number of books they sell, while attributing their failures to the deplorable decline of civilisation in general and the state of education in particular. At best, they do as they are being told by writers, who rightly or—more often—wrongly think they know perfectly well themselves how their work should be handled, promoted and sold.

Most publishers who played a role in Oscar Wilde's writing life are no exception to this generic pattern. His first publisher, David Bogue, based at St. Martin's Place near Trafalgar Square, functioned as little more than a printer, producing Wilde's debut collection of some sixty poems in 1881 in 750 copies under the more practical than poetic title, *Poems*. This was done at the author's expense and strictly following his typographical instructions. The print-run was divided in three editions of 250 copies each, so that the author, who was entirely in control of publicity for the book and did so with verve, sending out inscribed copies of the little book to illustrious authors and politicians of his day, could soon boast that his debut was already going through multiple reprints.

Throughout his career as a writer, up to his last long poem *The Ballad of Reading Gaol* which came out in 1898, Wilde remained very directive in his wishes for the fonts, layout, cover design and choice of paper and material for the binding. Most of his publishers were small firms, such as Osgood, McIlvaine & Co, The Bodley Head and Leonard Smithers. In one of his more acid letters to Messrs. Elkin Mathews and John Lane of The Bodley Head, Wilde with mock generosity concedes: 'There is no objection to publishers reading the works they produce before publication.' For John Lane the writer had even so little regard that he named the butler in his play *The Importance of Being Earnest* after him. On the other hand, Wilde had the greatest possible interest in a young employee at that same publishing house named Edward Shelley, who was later to testify against him during his criminal trials.

The fact that Wilde never occupied a regular place as an author on the list of the bigger English publishers during his lifetime (such as Macmillan, who published the works of Walter Pater and John Pentland Mahaffy, for example), was not so much due to the daring and idiosyncratic character of his personality—publishers did not shun a certain publicity profile even then—but rather to the fact that Wilde did not really occupy a position in the literary or academic establishment and that he initially wrote books mainly for an audience of connoisseurs: poetry, essayistic dialogues on art, historical tragedies and *Salome*, a Biblical drama translated from the French in which he originally wrote it. These were hardly the kind of titles that larger, increasingly internationally oriented commercial publishers would handle, especially from a writer who was still in the process of making his name among the general reading public.

It was not until 1891 that Oscar Wilde would publish a book that could be marketed as a novel in terms of character and scope, and this was done by the firm of Ward, Lock & Co, founded in 1854, which in recent years had also opened offices in New York and Melbourne. *The Picture of Dorian Gray*, which would remain Wilde's only novel and would become his most famous literary work, was originally written not as a novel but as a magazine story. It was only after the publication of that magazine version that the author reworked his tale about the young Dorian Gray, who sells the soul of his youth to the devil, into a fully-fledged novel, with almost twice as many chapters and various added storylines. In this process of 'novelisation' the writer also subdued some of the more explicit homosexual undertones in the story, in addition to the editorial cuts of some 500 words that had already been made by the editors of the magazine version, but to no avail. The novel would cause a scandal anyway as an immoral and transgressive work, despite the writer's claim in an added preface: 'There is no such thing as a moral or an immoral book. Books are well written or badly written. That is all.'

The original version of *Dorian Gray*, which appeared in the July 1890 issue of *Lippincott's Monthly Magazine*, went back to an initiative of the American publisher, Joseph M. Stoddart. It was he who approached two young English writers of his choice to write a story for the new British version of his magazine. To make sure that they would accept, he not only offered them a generous fee, but Stoddart personally travelled to England and invited them both for a special dinner, which took place on the 30th of August, 1889, at The

Langham Hotel on Portland Place, one of the best hotels in London. One writer was Oscar Wilde, whom the publisher remembered well from their successful collaboration during Wilde's American lecture tour seven years earlier, the other was a young medical doctor with literary aspirations by the name of Arthur Conan Doyle, who was just then starting out as a writer of historical novels and detective stories.

What would a person not give for the possibility of a cunningly placed recording device to eavesdrop on that dinner conversation? This meeting—immortalised as 'The Golden Evening' on a plaque next to the entrance of the still-existing Langham Hotel—was certainly one of the literary highlights of Stoddart's career. So would this publisher perhaps have put his memories of the evening on paper? For the purpose of this book, that would be quite convenient. As a matter of fact, it is far from inconceivable that he did so. Now that I think about it a little longer, it is even quite likely. And if such notes do indeed exist, then Stoddart's written impressions of the evening would undoubtedly have ended up in his personal archive. Yes, it all fits neatly, and I can now see the document clearly before my mind's eye.

12

TWO STORIES

*From the personal archive of
Joseph Marshall Stoddart (1845–1921)
(Van Pelt-Dietrich Library, Historical Society
of Pennsylvania, Closed Stacks Zp. 312-86.F)*

*[Stationery of the Westminster Hotel,
23-24 Leinster Gardens]*

London, 30th/31st of August 1889

'We say...,' said Oscar Wilde, and with his right hand he made a circling gesture in the air, like a magician who will pull out a playing card or a fluttering white dove from his sleeve at any moment, 'we say that a state is ruined by a battle. That is not so. A state is ruined by the general conditions which makes its safety depend on a battle.'

As Wilde's hand descended again and picked up his wine glass between thumb and forefinger, I saw Doyle hesitate. All evening he had been visibly impressed by

Arthur Conan Doyle around 1889, the year
of 'The Golden Evening'

Wilde's flow of words, which seemed to be able to bring
any subject to life. Before, the conversation was about
the Battle of Marathon, a subject about which Wilde
appeared very well informed indeed, having person-
ally visited the plain where the battle took place. It had
been the same earlier in the evening when it came to
Ravenna's mosaics, the effects of ingesting opium or
the imminent revolution in women's fashion. Wilde
seemed to be equally at home in every subject and
always knew how to formulate his observations and
opinions with ease and authority.

'But sometimes...,' Doyle began, 'the reverse is
true, and the fate of a battle and that of a nation
can coincide perfectly.' He paused for a moment and
looked at Gill and me in turn, and then at Wilde again.
'The Battle of Sedgemoor, to take an English example,
was a crystal-clear case of a self-affirming victory
for James II's Catholic England. The performance of
well-organised, well-trained, and well-armed troops
on the battlefield fully reflected the national fortunes
of the country.' Doyle did not dare to look triumphant
at this objection, yet I could see from the twinkling
look in his eyes that he thought he had made a point.

'My dear Doyle,' Wilde responded without a
moment's hesitation, 'that is one of the problems of
history: for every lesson you learn from the past, usually the opposite is also true.'

Delightful. All four of us had a good laugh about it,
and while a waiter took away our soup plates to make
room for the main course, I was enjoying myself to the
full. With the same deep satisfaction, I am now sitting
in my hotel room making some notes based on my
still-fresh memories. It is past midnight, and it has
been a few hours since I said goodbye to my precious
company, and yet I simply don't want the evening to
end or to go to bed. Above all, I do not want the events
of the past few hours to disappear completely into
oblivion. Tomorrow I will no doubt have forgotten the
precise wording of our table discussion, a wonderful
quote or the details of an after-dinner story.

The business arrangements we made towards
the end of the evening are unambiguous enough, but

what I want to secure for myself is the human side, the talents, the stories that made this evening an unforgettable experience. Until now, I have never kept a diary in my life, although as a publisher I have gone through many interesting encounters and experiences over the years. This evening, I'm sure, deserves to be recorded in a few personal notes. Who knows, I may benefit from it in later years, in case I ever decide to write my memoirs.

I am a Philadelphia man, and I like to run a business my own way. Agreements are agreements. And if agreements are violated, I will not rest until my interests are safeguarded, if necessary, by legal means. I have proven that in the past, right up to the Supreme Court! However, this here is not Philadelphia, not even America. This is England and that is a relatively new territory for me. Nevertheless, everything indicates that this will be a promising experiment.

However, I must get used to the English way of doing things. In the privacy of these notes, let me confess that I find them generally unfathomable, the English, so reserved and indirect in their way of speaking and therefore difficult to deal with in business matters. That is the nice thing about Oscar Wilde, who just speaks out and doesn't hold anything back, and he's also fully willing to try anything. I treasure the best memories of our collaboration during his tour in America and Canada about seven years ago. In the beginning, for his part, he had to get used to the American public, but within a month he got the hang of it and managed to give the people what they came for in all those lecturing halls and at countless receptions and dinners: to be stunned and amused. 'The greatest sin is boredom,' I once heard him say after such an evening, and as a publisher of books and magazines, I can only agree.

That was one of the reasons why in making my English plans for Lippincott's Magazine *I immediately thought of Wilde. And the whole idea of a separate British edition also came from my reading of* A Study in Scarlet, *which I discovered quite soon after publication last year and which I am still impressed with. Young Doyle—or, as he calls himself: Conan Doyle—succeeds in turning the workings of a mind, namely that of his detective Sherlock Holmes, into a character in a story. Such an idea fascinates me. Because that is the most difficult thing there is, as many years of dealing with writers have taught me: to make the intellectual thing entertaining, to present interesting ideas in an attractive way, so that a line of reasoning can be enjoyed as if it were an anecdote. I don't know if I'm explaining it in the best possible way, but when I come across it somewhere, I recognise it immediately. Edgar Allan Poe was a master of it, and Arthur Conan Doyle, as young as he is, has that same talent in him. I mean, speaking the truth and telling a story at the same time. To me, that is the essence of why a person should want to read a book. Not mere science, the domain of facts, nor merely fantasy, which, by its very nature is not connected to anything useful. No, a combination of both, so that there is no longer any difference between the pleasure of reading and the usefulness of learning.*

'*You have been in Afghanistan, I perceive,*' *says Sherlock Holmes, when he meets Dr Watson* M.D. *for the very first time in* A Study in Scarlet. *The reader is just as stunned as the sympathetic, not-too-clever doctor, who is soon sharing an apartment on Baker Street with the eccentric sleuth. When the reasoning behind that greeting is explained a few pages later, it is crystal clear and has the power of a revelation, in the same way as some of Oscar Wilde's short stories and fairy tales. So, in addition to Wilde, I wanted to involve young Doyle in my plans, and it was my old acquaintance Thomas Gill who suggested that they be invited together one evening, after which I in turn asked him to join me as my third guest. And so it happened that the four of us had dinner tonight.*

To make the seriousness of my intentions clear to both writers, I booked a table in the restaurant of The Langham Hotel on Portland Place, where I had eaten a truly excellent meal with guests twice before. Maybe it is because the proprietor of that hotel is an American, or because the entrance and courtyard are electrically lit, but as soon as I get out of my carriage in front of The Langham and walk up the steps to the entrance, I somehow feel as a Philadelphia man like I'm coming home. That the hotel's staff manages to be so obliging that it almost comes across as condescending is the price an American has to pay for British hospitality, as Oscar Wilde remarked as we walked to our table.

We sat in a corner of the restaurant, by a window that overlooks a spacious light court where palm trees stand in huge pots, as if we were not in the middle of

London, but somewhere in Bombay or in Cairo. On our table were two candlesticks with lighted candles that gave an almost wintry cosiness to this August evening. Gill proved himself to be a natural when it came to stimulating and directing the table conversation. Or was the conversation going so smoothly because we felt so comfortable as outsiders among ourselves: two native Irish, one Scotsman and one American together on English soil. Strangers in a strange land!

We certainly had no shortage of subjects. Doyle, who, like Wilde, is married and has been a father for several years, talked about his work as a GP in South-sea near Portsmouth, which leaves him more time for writing than he had counted on, after his many years of medical study. His lengthy historical novel Micah Clarke, *which honestly, I have only read in part, and which fascinated me less after* A Study in Scarlet, *has earned him some fine reviews, but not yet the success he hopes for. That was exactly the opportunity I needed to urge him to write another Sherlock Holmes-adventure for* Lippincott's. *At first, he did not seem too enthusiastic, although I think he understands how the promise of success comes with its own necessities, which a writer—especially one with a young family to support—cannot contravene with impunity.*

What else did we talk about? About Paris, about the future of warfare, about Oxford, about Dublin, about the differences in furnishing between American and English homes, about hand-reading, spiritism, about the difference between the creative and the applied arts, the role of cricket and other sports in university life, Roman Catholicism and the religion of the ancient Greeks. Regardless of the subject, Oscar Wilde had his factual knowledge and personal observations at the ready, often in the form of small, seemingly improvised tales, rhetorical displays, and invariably ending with a surprising symbolic bit of wisdom.

Our conversation was still flourishing, when the cheese was put on the table, accompanied by a tasty port wine. Guests were beginning to leave the restaurant in small groups, so it was high time for me to get down to business. A fee of one hundred pounds sterling for a story of approximately 45,000 words, that is the agreement in principle I made with each of them, and we toasted with the port wine. Of course, it remains to be seen whether they will both be able to honour their commitments, and what exactly they will hand in, and when.

My editorial experience told me not to set too strict a term for the delivery, but I expressed the hope that they will have their stories ready within two or three months, so that they can be included in the new British Lippincott's *early next year. Doyle, despite his personal preference for historical fantasies, seemed inclined to have his old hero Sherlock Holmes perform again, but exactly what Wilde is up to, he did not yet reveal. With his own experience as editor of* Woman's World, *he fully knows how difficult it is to make definite agreements for new contributions of which not even one word has yet been written.*

Speculating on possible topics gradually brought the evening to a close. Thanks to my good friend Gill

*this developed into a perfect highlight. Over coffee, he
asked the two writers for a small after-dinner story
as a farewell, he called it 'an anecdotal chocolate that
would give us an aftertaste of the evening.' Wilde left
the honour to begin to Doyle:*

*'We spoke earlier,' Doyle started, surveying the
table and the traces of our elaborate dinner, 'about
the Battle of Sedgemoor, which was fought on the
6th of July, 1685. I happened to look into this when I
was working on my novel* Micah Clarke, *about which
Mr Wilde made such kind remarks just now. The
Protestant rebel James Scott, first Duke of Monmouth
and illegitimate son of Charles II, was defeated in that
battle, and many hundreds of his poorly armed and
irregular troops were killed or captured by the Royal
English army. Monmouth himself managed to escape
the battlefield by exchanging clothes with a local
farmer. For nine days the Royals could not trace his
whereabouts, while in the meantime hundreds of his
imprisoned men were executed for high treason, some
by hanging, others by quarters. Monmouth managed
to reach the coast at Portsmouth, and perhaps hoped
to escape by sea, but on the tenth day, while hiding
in a ditch at the foot of an ash tree, he was spotted
and betrayed by a woman from a neighbouring farm.
He was severely weakened, for in ten days he had
eaten nothing but what he had been able to steal from
vegetable gardens along the way. He was immediately
arrested and taken to the Tower of London, where on
the 15th of July a huge crowd of people gathered for the
spectacle of his execution.'*

Doyle paused for a moment and took a sip of his port, looking at us in turn. It was a lurid story, so soon after our meal, Still, all three of us sat listening like little children to a bedtime fairy tale.

'The crowd was restless, partly from all too human bloodthirst, partly out of protest against this execution. Monmouth greeted his executioner, a villain named John Ketch, with the following words: "Here are six guineas. My servant will give you six more, if you do your job right in one go." Despite that generous reward, the executioner failed at the first blow, and to the fury of the screaming crowd, Ketch had to chop no less than five times and even had to use a knife until the head was completely separated from the body and James Scott, the first Duke of Monmouth, had given up the ghost as a martyr for the Protestant faith.

'Not long ago, gentlemen, I walked from Bournemouth as a pilgrim to Portsmouth to visit the coastal site called Christchurch, where the Duke of Monmouth was betrayed in 1685. And I can tell you that along the ditch where he hid during the very last days of his life, there still stands that same ash tree, with countless inscriptions scratched into its bark. The Duke's Protestant followers have left these marks over the years to honour their fallen leader. Dear friends, like that tree, a book is also a living carrier of histories, to which later readers pay their respects and to which they feel connected as a part of their lives. Just as the followers of Monmouth have scratched their names and messages into that tree, so readers write their names on the endpaper of our books. May we enjoy *that pleasure many times over, especially in our future cooperation. For now, I say in conclusion: thank you for the splendid hospitality enjoyed tonight.'*

The three of us gently patted the tabletop as a sign of our appreciation for this impromptu story, a historical parable of authorship, and while Doyle leaned back, we looked expectantly at Oscar Wilde.

'That was an exquisite story, as nasty as it was nice,' he began. 'Let me add to that a brief Persian legend, which is also possessed of a certain cruelty.' Wilde's gaze was a little dreamy, whether on account of the wine or from looking down some inner vista to discern the distant details of the fable he started to tell us.

'Bahram V was the cruel ruler of the Sassanid people, and he was a great bow hunter. He could fatally strike a fleeing gazelle from a galloping horse, regardless of his angle. This Bahram V had a favourite daughter who had reached marriageable age, but none of the candidates who came to ask for her hand found approval in her father's eyes. Again and again, they were rejected by the demanding king as unfit and unworthy. And so the princess languished day after day in the palace of the capital Ctesiphon, while her father was often away on one of his gazelle hunting parties.

'Now the princess had a slave girl, whom the Sassanids had captured in a battle against the Romans, after they had sacked her city and massacred or enslaved a large part of the population. This slave girl thought of a ruse to avenge herself for her imprisonment in the palace. She suggested to her mistress to make the following proposal to her father: "Allow me, O

Lord, to choose a secret word every day, and the one of
my marriage candidates who guesses the correct word
of the day will be allowed to marry me, for he will have
proved himself the smartest and the wisest of all men."'

Wilde looked around for a moment. The restaurant
was now almost completely deserted. We sat mesmer-
ised. On our table, the candles in the candlesticks had
shrunk to stubs. On the other side of the glass, the
palm leaves in the now dim light court hung down like
large tentacles. In that subdued light, Wilde continued.

'One evening Bahram V came back from the hunt
with a male gazelle that he had killed by shooting the
antlers from his head, so that it seemed as if the ani-
mal had now become female instead of male. With that
feat, he had won a bet with one of his younger brothers, and he was in a splendid mood, so he agreed to his
favourite daughter's proposal.

'After the announcement of this official decision,
which would provide the daughter of Bahram V with
the brightest and most promising marriage candidate,
young men from all over the empire came daily to
guess the word of the day during the afternoon audience. Very soon, Bahram V regretted his permission for
this contest, and he ordered that any candidate who
entered a wrong word would henceforth be thrown
directly into jail. Nevertheless, the daily flow of candidates continued, so renowned was the beauty of the
princess. The prisons of the country soon overflowed.

'It was then that the princess's slave carried out the
next stage of her nefarious plan. One morning she suggested to her mistress to choose as the word of the day

"crucifix," a word she remembered from her childhood
in her hometown in Asia Minor and which she knew
was an undesirable Christian symbol among the Sassanids. After the princess agreed to this idea, the slave
girl snuck out of the palace veiled. Outside the walls
of the city, she convinced the first young goatherd she
met that he had a chance to win the princess's hand,
if he said "crucifix" as the word of the day that same
afternoon during the audience in the main hall of
the palace.

‘As soon as the princess heard the ragged boy with
his stick utter the word "crucifix" that afternoon, she
judged inexorably, as she had done on all previous
days: "Wrong," and the young goatherd was taken
to prison floundering and screaming. That night the
princess said to her slave, "I saw you looking at him. Is
he your little friend or did you come up with this plan
out of revenge? You do not have to tell me, but from
now on I think you should remember one thing: that
every truth consists of a thousand little lies, just as
every lie can contain many a truth."’

‘With that lesson learned, the slave-girl continued
her drab existence in the palace. And the princess? She
was soon given in marriage by her father to an elderly
uncle, so that in later years she sometimes wondered
whether she would not have been better off with an
illiterate young goatherd as a husband.’

I have recorded Wilde's fairy tale to the best of my
abilities, although I wish my memory were more

accurate and reliable. There was also a brief scene involving a starry night, but unfortunately I can no longer remember the details. Perhaps I will ask Thomas Gill about it. Anyway, after saying goodbye to Wilde and Conan Doyle in front of the hotel, Gill and I stood and savoured what this August evening had brought us, and in the soft coolness the two of us continued the conversation a little while longer. There was not a single cloud in the dark evening sky.

After dropping Gill off at his house on the way, I drove on to my hotel at Leinster Gardens. Now it is a quarter past two. In the hotel and in the rest of the street complete silence reigns. Even the deep rumbling of the Underground line that audibly runs underneath here stopped some time ago. In the hope that with these words I have managed to preserve some of the enchantment of the previous evening, I am now going to bed, a happy publisher and a happy person. After an evening like this, as far as I'm concerned, there is no difference between the two.

13

STATIONS OF
THE CROSS

I.

When the young solicitor Jonathan Harker in Bram Stoker's novel *Dracula* travels to the castle of the bloodthirsty count in Transylvania, a small crucifix is hung around his neck by a woman who is sympathetic to him, to serve as a talisman against the calamities that await him. And indeed, as soon as the count grabs the young man's neck in the next chapter to throw himself at it with his fangs, and his fingers touch the beads of the chain on which the cross hangs, Dracula recoils. Later in the story, this incident prompts Harker to praise the miraculous power of the crucifix: 'Bless that good, good woman, who hung the crucifix round my neck! for it is a comfort and a strength to me whenever I touch it. It is odd that a thing which I have been taught to regard with disfavour and as idolatrous should in a time of loneliness and trouble be of help. Is it that there is something in the essence of the thing itself, or that it is a medium, a tangible help, in conveying memories of sympathy and comfort?'

The symbol of the small golden crucifix reappears several times in the novel. For example, when one of the female characters is being menaced, the learned Amsterdam vampire fighter Van Helsing steps forward: 'The professor held up his little golden crucifix, and said with wonderful calmness:— "Do not fear, my dear. We are here; and whilst this is close to you no foul thing can approach."'

It is quite tempting to assume that Bram Stoker, with the frequent use of this symbol in his novel, consciously or unconsciously refers to the golden cross that Oscar Wilde gave to Florence Balcombe on the 25th of December, 1876. Such things cannot be proved, of course, but it is worth trying out, in the way that from a box of keys you choose one that just might fit on a locked cupboard door.

II.

By the time Bram Stoker actually started writing *Dracula* in 1895, he had been married to Florence Balcombe for seventeen years. As we have seen, the marriage had been a rather hasty affair, after Bram had fallen under the spell of the great Henry Irving, who offered him a job in London. For Stoker, it was this opportunity that enabled him to propose to Florence. There was not much time to arrange everything—the farewell to his old job, the wedding, the removal—so Florence's swift departure from Dublin with her new husband left Oscar Wilde quite flummoxed, saying he had not seen this coming at all.

Soon after, Oscar also moved to London, followed by his mother. He would remain interested in his Florrie for a long time, for example having a bouquet delivered anonymously to her years later, when she had a rare stage performance as an actress. It seems that the feeling of might-have-been about their youthful infatuation, of which the small golden crucifix was a symbol, continued to play a role in the background of both their minds.

III.

Oscar Wilde's *The Picture of Dorian Gray* first appeared in the form of a long story on the 20th of June, 1890, in the July issue of *Lippincott's Monthly Magazine.* That is five years before the Viennese physician Sigmund Freud and his colleague Josef Breuer published the book *Studien über Hysterie.* In that study, psychological problems were explained for the first time with the concept of the subconscious. In later publications, Freud developed his ideas into a complete theory of the subconscious, in which he distinguished three domains: the *Es*, the *Ich* and the *Über-Ich.* It is interesting how clearly the features of this Freudian theory can be illustrated by the three main characters from Oscar Wilde's story, published years earlier. The beautiful young Dorian Gray is the *Ich*, the ego that seeks its way between his lower instincts and the demands placed on him by his origin and background. The *Es* is Lord Henry Wotton, who personifies the pleasure principle, wrapped in aphorisms that are as seductive as they are dangerous. And the painter Basil Hallward, who produces the portrait of Dorian Gray with which the whole story begins, is the Über-Ich, the Super-Ego, the moral educational body that (in this case unsuccessfully) tries to keep the ego on the right path, and who has to pay the highest price for his failed efforts.

Such Freudian interpretations can also be applied to Bram Stoker's novel *Dracula*, published in 1897. The book is almost exploding with sexual and especially homosexual innuendo, depictions of depravity, physical threat and violations, as well as oral and genital sexual symbolism. Vampirism, after all, is a kind of sexual activity without genitals, in which nevertheless all phenomena of sexual desire play a role, such as sucking, biting, moaning, physical submission, the desire to overpower and the concomitant urge to possess the other, and yes, to penetrate them, namely with the canines. In Freudian terms the morbid fear of the vampire can undeniably be interpreted as arising from repressed sexual desires.

IV.

One of the sources from which Bram Stoker says he derived the basic idea for his novel *Dracula* was the nightmare he had in the spring of 1890, referenced earlier, in which a girl tries to kiss a young man, not on the lips, but in his neck, until an old nobleman intervenes and exclaims in diabolical rage, 'This man belongs to me. I want him.'

Wilde, for his part, did not have to look far for the idea of a hidden painted portrait that forms the counterpart of a wandering protagonist. The classic horror novel *Melmoth the Wanderer* (1820), written by a brother-in-law of Wilde's maternal grandfather, contains the very same premise, although it is not the pursuit of forbidden pleasures with impunity that is at stake there, but the search for eternal life. The appearance of *The Picture of Dorian Gray* immediately caused a major scandal, with accusations against the writer of immorality and the glorification of indecent behaviour.

Dracula, however, written in the form of letters, diary entries, reports and telegrams, initially received a much calmer reception. One could argue that the lurid suggestiveness of

Stoker's book, with its detailed descriptions of blood-sucking vampires and child-luring graveyard spirits, entered the collective consciousness of his time much more insidiously. The young solicitor Jonathan Harker, held in the Transylvanian castle of the perverted Count Dracula, who in turn leaves his native land for England accompanied by big chests of earth to aid him in his perfidious activities, the sleepwalking Lucy Westenra who is weakened by nocturnal vampire attacks, turning her into a blood-sucking monster herself, the Amsterdam doctor Professor Van Helsing, who tries to defuse the monsters by performing blood transfusions and using wreaths of garlic flowers and a golden crucifix: the nightmarishness of what happens to all these and other main characters stands in stark contrast to the cool, documentary style in which the novel is written, almost like a clinical report on everything that was whirling around in the author's haunted mind.

The fact that Count Dracula, to Jonathan Harker's bewilderment, turns out not to have a mirror image and cannot be portrayed by painters, can be symbolically interpreted as a lack of any human self-reflection, a fact that in its turn is mirrored by Dorian Gray's portrait, stored away in his attic, so that he does not have to see the traces of misbehaviour on his painted face. From this point of view, it seems as if Dorian Gray and Count Dracula are connected by some kind of kinship, and on closer inspection there is a lot to be said for that. At least that is true of their spiritual fathers.

V.

Apart from their rival relationship with Florence Balcombe, Oscar Wilde and Bram Stoker had much in common on a personal level. They both studied at Trinity College Dublin, although after three years Wilde left for Oxford on a scholarship. Stoker was seven years older, but as fellow-Dubliners and as fellow-students, they knew each other pretty well. Stoker even liked coming to the house of Wilde's parents, and it is probably there that he first met Florence Balcombe. She must have been eighteen or nineteen at the time and was still the object of Oscar's love interest.

Both men paid special attention in their lives and in their work to the supernatural, the world of folklore and fairy tales, and most of all to the theatre: at the beginning of his career Stoker wrote dramatic reviews for the *Dublin Evening Mail*, just as Oscar Wilde would start his career a few years later by writing reviews and art criticism for the *Dramatic Review*, the *Pall Mall Gazette* and many other papers and magazines.

Outwardly, Stoker and Wilde seem to have been different types: Stoker with his full beard and moustache and a childish, somewhat uncertain expression, Wilde with his often half lured eyes, his full lips and his carefully thought-out hairstyle. But they were the same height (6-foot 2in), almost a head taller than most people at the time, such as Florence Balcombe who was 5-foot 8in. What they also had in common as young men was their admiration for the enormous personality of the then forty-year-old Shakespearean actor Henry Irving. Wilde admired Irving for his impressive acting career that included famous roles as Shylock, Macbeth, Hamlet and Faust, and he dedicated some of his poems to him.

Stoker's admiration for Irving went much further: for him the actor was an object of total and slavish veneration, as evidenced by the two-volume book *Personal Reminiscences of Henry Irving*, which Stoker would publish a year after the death of the great actor. Stoker's many descriptions of Irving's highly expressive and even grotesque manner of performing convey a stage personality of diabolical force. This had led some people to speculate that it was Irving who was Stoker's model for Count Dracula. But even if this character was indeed based on a single person in real life, there are other strong candidates to consider.

VI.

In addition to Irving, the first English actor ever to be elevated to the peerage, there is another impressive male personality, who not only enjoyed Oscar Wilde's special admiration, but who also exercised an enormous attraction on the young Bram Stoker: Walt Whitman. Shortly after he had discovered an English anthology from *Leaves of Grass* and became, in his own words, 'a lover of Walt Whitman,' the twenty-four-year-old Stoker wrote a letter to his new idol, which certainly for its time can be called unusually candid:

'If you are the man I take you to be you will like to get this letter,' Stoker begins his epistle, which was first published by Stoker-biographer David J. Skal (*Something in the Blood: The Untold Story of Bram Stoker, The Man Who Wrote* Dracula, 2016). Stoker writes of himself: 'I am six feet two inches high and twelve stone weight naked and used to be forty-one or forty-two inches around the chest.' Then on Whitman's poems: 'I have read your poems with my door locked late at night.' And a little further on: 'But be assured of this, Walt Whitman—that a man of less than half your own age [...] felt his heart leap towards you across the Atlantic and his soul swelling.' He admits that he has told more about himself than ever to anyone else, but as he remarks, more to himself than to Whitman: 'How sweet a thing it is for a strong healthy man with a woman's eyes and a child's wishes to feel that he can speak to a man who can be if he wishes father, brother and wife to his soul.' Stoker concludes the 1400-word letter with the confession: 'I thank you for all the love and sympathy you have given me in common with my kind.'

After completing this remarkable confession, Stoker initially did not dare to send it. It was not until four years later that he put it in the post, together with a new letter, in which he mentions that he has felt, thought and suffered much in the intervening years 'and I can truly say that from you I have had much pleasure and much consolation.' Three weeks later he received an answer from his great idol, which must have made him unspeakably happy from the very first words: 'My dear young man,— Your letters have been most welcome to me...'

VII.

Two years after Oscar Wilde together with Joseph Stoddart had visited his hero Walt Whitman at his home in Camden, New Jersey, it was Bram Stoker's turn, during Henry Irving's American *Hamlet*-tour in 1884, to finally press the hand of his distant male inspirer. Whitman was 'all that I had ever dreamed of, or wished for in him,' as he would later record. He visited him again a few years later, this time on a *Faust*-tour of Irving's, and he also writes about that meeting in the most intense terms: 'the memory of that room will never leave me.' Cultural historian Christopher Frayling (in his *Vampyres. Lord Byron to Count Dracula*, 1991) rightly called Bram Stoker 'a born hero worshipper.'

However one interprets the attitude to Whitman of both Wilde and Stoker (and indeed many other young men, such as the equally married and homosexual cultural critic and poet John Addington Symonds), and taking into account the entirely different terminology in which we today speak of homosexuality, bisexuality, queerness, non-binarity, and so on, it is clear that Florence Balcombe was completely excluded from all these intense, exclusively male sympathies of her husband. In addition to Henry Irving and Walt Whitman, Bram Stoker even had a third very intimate friend in the immensely popular writer Hal Caine, to whom *Dracula* would be dedicated: 'To my dear friend Hommy-Beg', so runs the printed dedication, the use of his pet-name giving this friendly tribute an especially cuddly effect. In the presentation copy for Caine, the author added by hand: 'from his loving friend / Bram Stoker / 25 May 1897.'

VIII.

The term 'homosexual' was not yet widely used in England in these years, certainly not as a noun. It was not until well into the 1890s that the separate concept of homosexuality would gradually come into focus, when theories and terminologies of the early German sexologists gained an international circulation outside the scientific community. In our time, at least in large parts of the Western world, after many decades of hard-fought decriminalisation, emancipation, liberation and unending shifting terminologies, the term 'homosexual' has become part of a wider sexual nomenclature, under which a person may individually determine the desired gender designation and the corresponding form of address.

The problem with correctly indicating the sexual identity of Oscar Wilde, Bram Stoker and so many others of their male contemporaries is that in their time the division

into two sexes and the choice between two sexual orienta-
tions was still unshakably established and that, moreover, no
distinction was made between sex and gender. On the one
hand, Wilde and Stoker were both married and father of one
or more children, while on the other hand, they harboured
affective, erotic or even outright sexual desires towards other
men. The heterosexually married state was the life visible
from the outside, the other took place in secret and did not
'dare to speak its name.'

IX.

In the case of Oscar Wilde, thanks to all the explicit details
that emerged during his trials, we know a little more about the
practicing side of his extramarital sexual activities, although
during his cross-examinations the prosecutor made sure that
a deliberately offensive version of his conduct would emerge.
Office assistants, valets, bellboys, newspaper vendors and
jobless young men of sixteen or a bit older, declared that in
private rooms of restaurants, in a male brothel or late at night
in hotel rooms, they had consented in mutual masturbation,
sometimes followed by anal penetration. For this they had
been rewarded with money and costly gifts, such as silver
cigarette cases and watches. A chambermaid of the Savoy
Hotel told the court that there had been a steady stream of
boys into Wilde's room at the hotel, and that his bedsheets
were often in a most disgusting state, with traces of vaseline,
soil and semen.

As far as Bram Stoker is concerned, it is virtually impossible more than a century after his death to ascertain what
exactly he did when with whom. One may well ask oneself
whether this sort of curiosity is even appropriate, but given

the criminal nature of such acts at the time and since our image of Florence Balcombe's life does in part depend on the kind of life her husband was leading, it is by no means irrelevant. In any case, Bram Stoker himself seems to have done everything to ensure that the private side of his life would be hidden from the world, so that at the most some of it becomes visible through the veil of his literary work.

Clearly, Stoker's youthful veneration for Walt Whitman shows strong homoerotic traits. Nor can it be denied that his relationship with Henry Irving in its utter submissiveness makes a slavish, almost masochistic impression. And his friendship with Hal Caine was so intense and emotionally complete that there seems to be almost no distinction between their friendship and feelings of mutual love. These male relationships, which were so crucially important to Stoker, cannot be described much more concretely than this, and perhaps it is better not to try to forcefully assign modern terms to them, which could lead to anachronistic labelling. What remains most intriguing, especially in connection with a search for Florence Balcombe's golden crucifix, is the relation between Bram Stoker and Oscar Wilde.

For Wilde, that relation was, in a sense, quite unambiguous. Stoker was a family and college friend from Dublin who had married the girl Oscar may at one time have thought he would marry himself. It had not turned out that way and Wilde, who had meanwhile married someone else, periodically resorted to a certain charm offensive. Thus he could show Florence how much he was living up to his talents as a journalist and writer and as an artistic man of the world, perhaps with the hidden message that he was certainly not inferior in success and prestige to the husband she had chosen over him. The couples Wilde and Stoker must have met often enough at receptions, first nights and other social occasions in the London theatre world. They even met a few times at parties in their mutual homes. For Wilde, who had admitted to his homosexual orientation soon after his marriage in 1884 (or perhaps earlier), Bram Stoker was not a significant factor in his life. Conversely, there was more to it than that.

X.

For Bram Stoker, Oscar Wilde was a former rival in love, who still showed an interest in his wife. Wilde was also a competitor in the theatre world, with the satirical plays that became spectacularly successful from the early '90s onwards, while Stoker, as dedicated manager of the Lyceum Theatre, carried out his financial and administrative work in the shadow of the great Henry Irving. Most confusing and disturbing of all: certainly from 1891, after his acquaintance with Lord Alfred Douglas, Wilde seemed to have found a way to give male camaraderie, the Whitmanian fraternisation with his friends, the open preference for male companionship—or whatever one wants to call it—a place in his life, both in private and in public. In this regard Stoker himself had made no progress at all.

This sharp contrast may suggest a psychological explanation for the curious fact that Bram Stoker does not mention the name of Oscar Wilde in any of his writings. Never, nowhere. Not in his letters nor in his posthumously published diary, not in his journalistic publications—not even in the highly autobiographical two-volume memoir about Henry Irving, that includes by name just about anyone who was anybody in the London cultural and theatrical world between 1880 and 1905.

Up to 1895 the reason for this remarkable silence was perhaps that in Stoker's eyes Wilde was still an old love rival and a competitor for the favour of the theatre public and the dramatic press. But Wilde's conviction and imprisonment in May 1895 may have instilled something quite different in Stoker, namely fear, or rather: pure panic. It is even said that at the time of Oscar Wilde's trials and his conviction, many practicing English gay men fled the country for shorter or longer periods of time. In any case, that goes for Lord Alfred Douglas.

XI.

Turning to literary studies, we are immediately confronted with a wave of journal articles that have washed over the sexual, gender and identitarian aspects of *Dracula* since the 1970s. In light of the theme of our search I am most impressed by two American journal articles, namely Christopher Craft, "Kiss Me with those Red Lips: Gender and Inversion in Bram Stoker's *Dracula*", published in *Representations*, No. 8 (Autumn, 1984), pp. 107-133, and Talia Schaffer, "A Wilde Desire Took Me. The Homoerotic History of *Dracula*", published in *English Literary History*, Vol. 61, No. 2 (Summer, 1994), pp. 381-425.

The thrust of these two startling analyses of Bram Stoker's novel is a reading of *Dracula* that is closely linked to the scandal surrounding the criminal trial of Oscar Wilde. In this interpretation, it was not the dominant Henry Irving who was the model for the 'haemosexual' Count Dracula (a striking adjective, coined by the English vampirologist Christopher Frayling) nor the bold Walt Whitman, with whom so many young men sought refuge, but none other than Oscar

Wilde. According to Clark and even more emphatically Schaffer, it is he who hides behind the menacing, and at the same time elusive figure of the vampire.

XII.

Although Bram Stoker had been preparing research and notes for *Dracula* (initially under the title *The Undead*) ever since his inspiring nightmare in March 1890, many characteristics of the repulsive count correspond to details from Wilde's criminal trial, and especially his practicing sexual life. Schaffer observes that the count's entire castle evokes the atmosphere and features of the pimp Alfred Taylor's male brothel—always closed curtains, no servants—as described in the courtroom. And the rules imposed on the imprisoned Jonathan Harker by his lurid host are strikingly similar to the restrictions that, according to press reports, applied to the imprisoned Oscar Wilde: giving up his clothes, his letters being censored, and so on.

Wilde was accused by the prosecutor of being a spoiler of public morals, the central figure in a circle of corruption, taking advantage of innocent boys. In sum, he was transformed in the public image into a kind of vampire, a transformation that was then further fictionalised by Bram Stoker, until we have an evil force who is out to create as many imitators as possible with his deadly urges, exerting a power as destructive as it is immortal. Craft and Schaffer persuasively show how Stoker made this publicly demonised version of Wilde into his diabolical protagonist.

Building on this hypothesis Nina Auerbach, in her study *Our Vampires, Ourselves* (Chicago, 1995), even suggests that Stoker's language in *Dracula* liberally adapts the idiom of

Oscar Wilde's love letters to Lord Alfred Douglas, as read out by the prosecutor during his cross-examination of Wilde. For the wording of these declarations of love, Stoker could draw on the extensive press reports of the trials, while carefully omitting any explicit indication of the origin of these quotes.

And so in *Dracula* the hyperbolic Freudian inversion of someone who is deemed neither a man nor a woman and who threatens to multiply in his followers, is transformed into the nightmare of a man who is neither alive nor dead and who tries to turn his victims into new vampires. On a personal level Stoker's novel thus serves as a foil for the dilemma between secrecy and confession about his own sexual orientation, veils of imagination behind which he can continue to hide himself.

Oscar Wilde's sentence to two years' imprisonment with hard labour was dated the 24th of May, 1895. In those very same days, five years after the nightmare that had given him the basic idea for his novel, Bram Stoker put the first chapter of *Dracula* to paper. While Wilde disappeared into prison, Stoker's alter ego Jonathan Harker was locked up in Dracula's Transylvanian book-castle. Talia Schaffer concludes that *Dracula* is a novel that 'explores Stoker's fear and anxiety as a closeted homosexual man during Oscar Wilde's trial.'

The novel was published eventually on the 26th of May, 1897, a few days after Oscar Wilde, having completed his two years' imprisonment with hard labour, had been released and had left the country, going straight into exile to France.

XIII.

With all these adventurous and far-reaching literary theories, one cannot help feeling some degree of pity for poor Florence Balcombe. First her courtship by Wilde was brief and anti-climactic, since she was almost immediately—perhaps unintentionally—left to her own devices. Then marriage to Bram Stoker obliged her to tolerate the competition of several all-embracing male friendships, while his constant absence left her to raise their son virtually alone. And that is even without taking the speculations about a syphilis infection of both young men into account.

The accusations, as they can be found in various sources, that Florence was deficient in her marital love for Bram, that after the birth of her only son she became averse to sexual intercourse with her husband, and that she was a frigid woman anyway, seem textbook examples of adding insult to injury.

XIV.

Just as Count Dracula is defused at various points in Bram Stoker's novel by means of a small golden crucifix, Florence Balcombe, for her part, sought solace at the cross. In 1904—four years after Oscar Wilde's deathbed conversion—she herself went over to the Roman Catholic Church. Did she at that time still have Oscar's little golden crucifix in her possession? Had Bram Stoker ever seen the thing, maybe even around her neck, when she was still Oscar's girl? She will probably never have worn the jewel openly after her marriage. Had she long ago returned the cross to Wilde, in accordance with his urgent request, so that it lay for years as a symbol of their shared past somewhere in the house at No. 16 Tite Street, waiting for the fatal destruction of Wilde's entire existence as a writer and as a human being? Or had she hidden it somewhere, if only to pull it out occasionally in lonely moments, when Bram was away on one of his lengthy tours with Henry Irving?

14

VISIT

On the 25th of October, 1993, the American actor and art collector Vincent Price—full name Vincent Leonard Price Jr.—passed away. He was born in 1911 in St. Louis, Missouri as the youngest of four children. His father, Vincent Leonard Price Sr., was the son of Vincent Clarence Price, the inventor of *Dr. Price's Baking Powder*, a goldmine that permitted Vincent Jr., upon finishing high school, to do whatever he wanted with his life. Price's first act was to embark on an extensive journey across the European continent, after which he enrolled in the prestigious Yale University, majoring in English and Art History.

Once his bachelor's degrees were in his pocket, Price left for London to pursue a master's in fine arts at the Courtauld Institute. But as always, when the possibilities in life are numerous, chance played a decisive role, and after replacing someone in the role of a gumchewing American policeman in a stage production entitled *Chicago*, he got into the theatre in England. After his return to the US and performing successfully in various roles on Broadway, he landed in Hollywood.

There, Price quickly became one of the most beloved actors in the horror genre. He played his first gruesome role in the historical murder drama *Tower of London* (1939), in which the part of the executioner was played by none other than Boris Karloff, who had gained fame for his portrayal of Frankenstein's monster and an Egyptian mummy brought back to life. Although Price also played many serious, historical, romantic and even comic theatre and film roles in his long career, both his face and in particular his voice are inextricably linked to the horror genre, from *The Invisible Man Returns* to *The Mad Magician* and from *House on Haunted Hill* to *The Fall of the House of Usher*, the first of a whole series of successful Edgar Allan Poe film adaptations in which he starred.

Price was also in great demand as a radio play actor. With his characteristic and unmistakable voice, he was able to suggest a perfect combination of inviting seductiveness and merciless bloodlust. His shrill, lugubrious laugh, which continues to sound posthumously from various sources on the internet, has frightened millions of people visiting the Phantom Manor at Disneyland Paris.

It is therefore no wonder that Price had a special affinity for Bram Stoker's *Dracula* and in 1982 he made a documentary under the tile *Vincent Price's Dracula: The Great Undead*, with himself playing the sinister host and suggestive commentator. The film portrays the entire history of the bloodthirsty Transylvanian Count on the basis of historical facts and film fragments, from the original legend, through Bram Stoker's key work, to a selection from the hundreds of 20th-century vampire films, including *Nosferatu* (1922), *Vampyr* (1932), *Mark of the Vampire* (1935), *Return of the Vampire* (1943) and *The Vampire* (1957). From an armchair by a deceptively cosy

Vincent Price in 1978 as Oscar Wilde in
the play Diversions and Delights

fire, Price also discusses the most probate methods to keep a vampire at bay, such as smearing the doorways and window sashes with fresh garlic and, most of all, holding up a Christian cross. 'Its shape has defended many a film star from the fangs of Dracula,' he explains with professional irony.

And yet despite all these associations with Bram Stoker's creation, the unlikely truth is that perhaps the most famous and successful theatre role Vincent Price ever played, was not Count Dracula, but Oscar Wilde. In a production entitled *Diversions and Delights*, written by film- and TV-screenwriter and playwright John Gay, Price starred as the fallen Irish writer in a more than hour-long solo performance. Supposedly speaking from a small Parisian theatre in November 1899, Price/Wilde looks back on his family background, his childhood, his education, his theatrical triumphs, his love for Lord Alfred Douglas, and his tragic fall as a result of 'the love that dare not speak its name.' Richly interspersed with Wildean epigrams and in a beautiful retrospective structure of his entire life story, the viewer gets to see and to hear Vincent Price in his ultimate performance, the role he was born to play.

The theatre press and the public certainly agreed, and after its premiere on the 11th of July, 1977, at the Marines' Memorial Theatre in San Francisco, a total of some 800 performances followed in more than 300 cities, in the US and as far as Australia. Unfortunately, there is only a poor audio recording of this performance and a short video fragment of some five minutes, which was recorded especially for an American TV-broadcast of the Dick Cavett Show.

Many actors have tried to portray Oscar Wilde as a character over the past hundred years, including such luminaries as Robert Morley, Klaus Maria Brandauer, Peter Finch, Rupert Everett and Stephen Fry. As to who succeeded best, the answer is of course subjective, depending on one's 'inner Oscar Wilde'. In any case to me those few minutes of Vincent Price have an exceptional appeal. How I would have loved to witness the premiere of the complete performance in San Francisco, but as the reader may remember, on the 11th of July, 1977, I was travelling with a friend in Greece.

Apparently, Price felt a special connection with both Bram Stoker and Oscar Wilde. Now I know the following sounds improbable, but you really have to take this from me, because when I am inventing something in this book, I always say so explicitly. Here it comes: the fact is that this same Vincent Price, twenty-four years old at the time and studying for his master's degree at the Courtauld Institute in London, was invited in November 1934, by a friend in the literary publishing business, to come to tea together with a few others at the home of none other than the now seventy-six-year-old Florence Balcombe. She lived at Kinnerton Studios, in one of those quiet *mews* behind the busy streets of London's posh Knightsbridge district.

More than twenty years had passed since Bram Stoker's demise. The death of Bram's lord and master Henry Irving— then *Sir* Henry—in 1905 had also meant the end of his job as business manager of the Lyceum Theatre. In his remaining years, and in spite of deteriorating health, Stoker had tried to maintain his relentless pace of work as a writer, now his only remaining source of income. Within a few years, this resulted in a rapid succession of a dozen new novels and collections of short stories, none of which, however, managed to match the appeal and success of *Dracula*. Even the addition 'By the author of *Dracula*' on the cover of the vampiristic novel *The Lady of the Shroud* (1909) was of no avail.

In *The Lair of the White Worm* (1910) Stoker tried once more to conjure the spirit of *Dracula* with myriad grotesque and slimy details. But the book, with a story that is as far-fetched as it is improbable, fails to capture the alchemy that gave the earlier novel its timeless appeal. The book is littered with cheap effects: poisonous black snakes, crates of live mongooses, mesmeric experiments and hidden pits under a house where lives a terrible white worm, at the end of the story destroyed by a colossal dynamite explosion, after which the male and female protagonist marry as an obligatory *happy ending.* For such stuff you probably have to be a born and insatiable lover of the horror-genre.

One of Stoker's last books was *Famous Impostors,* published in 1910, a non-fiction book that presents an overview of famous and lesser-known swindlers, con men, wizards, clairvoyants and other historical figures. Particularly curious is the section 'Women as Men,' in which the author gives a number of written portraits of women in history who have posed as men, culminating in an extensive chapter in which the theory is explored that Queen Elizabeth I was actually a man. Apparently, even at the end of his life, gender and sexuality were still very much on his mind. On the 20th of April, 1912, a few days after the sinking of the *Titanic,* Bram Stoker breathed his last, faithfully cared for by his wife until the very end. Speculation as to whether he had succumbed to the tertiary stage of syphilis would frequently resurface in the Stoker family and among biographers.

In the years that followed, Florence showed her strongest and most tenacious side when it came to caring for her late husband's literary work, of which she had inherited the copyright. She edited a posthumous collection of short stories (*Dracula's Guest and Other Weird Stories,* 1914), she actively corresponded with his old and new publishers at home and abroad and—most important of all—she undertook a veritable legal crusade against the producers of the German *Dracula* film adaptation by Friedrich Murnau under the title *Nosferatu* (1922). That film plays a crucial role in early European expressionist film history, but the producer neglected to arrange the rights properly, and Florence rightly felt robbed of the royalties due to her. After years of litigation in Germany, Florence was rewarded with a court ruling in her favour, that ordered all copies of the film to be withdrawn from the market and destroyed, a fate from which—fortunately for film history—a few copies escaped. Many other film adaptations and numerous translations of *Dracula* would follow. This bitter struggle for her rights as heiress earned Florence the nickname 'the widow of Dracula', as unjustified as it was unfortunate.

It was that widow's house that in November 1934 the student Vincent Price entered for an introduction and a cup of tea. Among the visiting party were the writer, adventurer and former radical MP Robert Cunninghame Graham, who had been a friend of Oscar Wilde and had corresponded with him even after his release from prison, and Axel Munthe, who had offered hospitality to Wilde and Douglas in his Villa San Michele on Capri in 1897, when they had been expelled from the Grand Hotel Quisisana after complaints from other English guests. So not only the ghost of Bram Stoker will have hung in the air that afternoon at Kinnerton Studios, but in particular also that of Oscar Wilde.

It had now been some sixty years since Wilde courted Florence Balcombe, but in her apartment the traces of that long-gone time were still tangibly present, according to the account that Vincent Price wrote of his visit many years later when asked about it by Stoker biographer David Skal. Price makes special mention of the portraits of the still youthful Florence that hung on the wall, painted by great artists of the English fin-de-siècle such as Edward Burne-Jones, Dante Gabriel Rossetti and Walter Osborne. Among these was also Oscar Wilde's drawn portrait of her, plus the watercolour with a loving dedication he gave her of the landscape at

Lough Corrib, the large lake in County Galway, Ireland, near his parents' holiday home.

Price also wrote an enthusiastic letter describing the visit to his family in the US ('the most wonderful things are all over the house'). Apparently, the atmosphere of the visit was so friendly that Florence showed her visitors around the house and perhaps also shared some of her correspondence with the now world-famous Oscar Wilde. Many years later, that bundle of letters would be sold off to a dealer by a second cousin of Bram Stoker, named Daniel Farson, who liked to go out drinking in Soho with the 'wild set' around artist Francis Bacon. In the end only six letters from Oscar to Florence have remained, while of course in a world without telephone and email, and being often far apart, they must have corresponded quite regularly.

It is more than tantalising to wonder where the little gold crucifix was at that moment. Could seventy-six-year-old Florence have kept this piece of jewellery all these years, that is to say if she had not given it back to Oscar after all? Had it long since been lost sometime during the many removals? Or perhaps in her old age Florence simply wore it around her neck, and Price saw it dangling there with his own eyes, not knowing what he was looking at. Unfortunately, I missed my opportunity to ask him, as Price was still living in the 80s and early 90s, when I was already working on Oscar Wilde and publishing articles about him. But Price passed away in 1993, as mentioned earlier, and it is now too late.

To the best of my knowledge, Vincent Price Jr. was the last possible living witness in connection with the quest I have undertaken in this book. Now that biographical or literary research apparently will not succeed in bringing back our little golden cross, all that remains is to call on the most intelligent and inventive sleuth of all time. I refer of course to Sherlock Holmes, Arthur Conan Doyle's creation, who came into the world as an exact contemporary of Oscar Wilde, both having been born in 1854. Who else could be more suitable, perhaps even destined, to clarify this matter? In any case, publisher Joseph M. Stoddart would have welcomed this final intersection of Conan Doyle and Wilde, the two writers he admired so much, if only in the realm of the imagination.

15

THE GOLDEN CRUCIFIX

'My dear Watson,' said Sherlock Holmes, who stood by
the fireplace tucking his pipe with some tobacco scraps
from the previous day, 'how does married life agree
with you?' I watched how his tawny figure was silhou-
etted by the grey morning light that entered the room
through the bay window. Although spring had already
produced a few fine days, it was now drizzling and the
temperature outside was quite low for the month of
April. Fortunately, a pleasant fire was burning in our
old sitting room on Baker Street.

From my familiar chair, I watched as Holmes,
dressed in his mouse-grey dressing gown, remained
busy by the mantelpiece. As soon as he had pressed
all the carefully dried tufts and wisps with his curved
index finger into his pipe, my friend turned to me,
and I saw the teasing twinkle in his eyes. Even at this
rather early morning hour, there was nothing sleepy
in that glance. As always, he had been awake for hours,

presumably engrossed in some chemical experiment, a study of traces or some other kind of analysis from which he could derive data for eliminating impossibilities or substantiating hypotheses in the solution of the puzzling cases presented to him by the most diverse clients.

'Oh, I quite like it,' I answered truthfully. Holmes sat down diagonally across from me in his chair and, as soon as he had lit his pipe, puffing and lightly smacking, a fragrant cloud of tobacco fumes encircled my former roommate's head. 'But now that Mary has left for her aunt early this morning for a few days,' I continued, 'your telegram was very timely, and it is certainly a pleasure to be here again in our old bachelor quarters. Fortunately, Anstruther was willing to take over some appointments with patients from me for the next few days.'

Holmes seemed unimpressed by my enthusiasm about married life, his half-lidded eyes showing that his concentrated attention was, if not with his own thoughts, then at least with the pleasurable taste of his morning pipe. For him, the whole concept of marriage was purely theoretical. What he disapproved of, was the irrationality of it, the abandonment of a carefully arranged existence of one's own, for an uncertain communality with someone one would never know as well as one knew oneself. In fact, the closest he had ever come to anything approaching marriage was when I had lived with him for some years, here at 221B Baker Street, after returning from Afghanistan. This practical experiment had gone remarkably well, and

*if at some point I had not met my dear Mary, Holmes
and I would probably have continued our bachelor life
together in these rented rooms in Marylebone to this
very day.*

*After Holmes exchanged his pipe for a plate with
ham and eggs that Mrs Hudson brought in, while I
eagerly embarked on a dish of curried chicken, we
talked for some time about the possible pleasures and
inevitable shortcomings of marital life, until Holmes
wiped his mouth and got to the point as to why he had
asked me by telegram to come round without delay.
From the breast pocket of his dressing gown, he fished
a folded note that he held out to me without comment.
The following text in jaunty handwriting was on it:*

London, 3 April 1895

Dear Mr Holmes,

*Being aware of your reputation for inventiveness and
your ability to solve seemingly incomprehensible problems,
I would like to visit you tomorrow at 10:30am to present
to you, on behalf of a good friend, an enigmatic matter
involving the happiness of several people. Thanking you
in advance for your kind interest,*

Respectfully,
Abraham Stoker
4 Durham Place, Chelsea

Before I had time to ask my friend for further explanation, he said: 'Of course a man cannot refuse such a request, although the letter writer is probably not entirely straightforward. But,' he added with a glance at the clock, 'that is something we can presently discuss with him, because I think I can already hear his footsteps at the front door.'

A few moments later, the burly figure of a man stepped into the room, his impressive stature accentuated by a full dark beard. The man was approximately six foot three and impeccably dressed. Yet in spite of his imposing appearance, he made a nervous and hurried first impression. He placed his hat on the small table by the door and, following Holmes's outstretched arm, lowered himself into the chair opposite the two of us. While Mrs Hudson took away the empty plates to her kitchen, our visitor declined our offers of hospitality. He stayed on the edge of his chair, as if he would get up at any moment to leave again, and he looked at me skittishly a few times.

Stoker clearly wanted to get to the point without delay, but Sherlock Holmes was ahead of him: 'Welcome, Mr Stoker. Rest assured that there is plenty of time for the topic you want to discuss. This is Dr Watson, who often assists me in my research, and we will be happy to try and help you. May I ask, if you are in such a hurry, why you did not let your carriage ride the last 200 yards, to our front door?'

Mr Stoker was visibly startled by this question. Holmes pointed to the hat Stoker had placed next to the door and explained that it had become visibly *wetter than might be expected from a brief pavement crossing, but that it would have been much more wet if Mr Stoker had walked all the way from his house.*

'I... I admit that I alighted a little way back in Baker Street, at the corner of Marelybone Road.'

'And did the pharmacy have the medicine your friend needs? Or do I take it that this too is actually intended for yourself?'

Under this display of sagacity, Mr Stoker leaned back into his chair, and after a deep sigh he spoke with some difficulty: 'I am afraid there is no point in trying to hide anything from you.'

'My dear Mr Stoker, it is not that difficult. Leaving your home you came here by carriage, and when you were almost at the right house number on Baker Street, you saw the pharmacy on the corner, and decided to get out and buy a sedative to calm your nerves. Otherwise, we would certainly have heard your carriage arriving at the door. In the pharmacy you had to wait longer than expected, so that in the end you had to hurry to be here on time for our appointment. Moreover, it is the faint air of disinfectant lingering in your clothes, which betrays the nature of your little purchase.'

I saw the somewhat cloudy and uncertain look in the intense blue eyes of Mr Stoker, who was visibly stunned by this line of reasoning, with which I have heard Sherlock Holmes impress his clients so many times. Frankly, it continues to amaze me, how the strictest application of rationality can paradoxically give the impression of pure sorcery or clairvoyance. As

*soon as Holmes explains his train of thought, I some-
times have the idea that next time I could do it myself,
but from repeated experience I have found that this is a
little too optimistic.*

*'We will be happy to try and help you with your
problem,' Holmes continued, 'but then it is indeed best
if you give us as many of the pure facts as possible. Let
us for the moment listen to you. Pray proceed.' While
he was speaking, Holmes had risen to put two more
blocks of wood on the fire and when he sat down again,
he picked up his clay pipe to concentrate all the better
on the story that awaited us.*

*'I'm sorry I was not completely honest in my note,
but at the moment I live under considerable strain.
Without sedatives, I would certainly not be able to keep
up with my busy professional life right now. I sleep
badly and I am very worried, especially about my wife.'*

*'You work in the theatre, if I am not mistaken?'
asked Holmes. The stacks of newspapers on either side
of his chair testified to the fact that he is always quite
well informed about what is going on in the social and
cultural life of the city, and I know from experience
that he even reads the reviews, the letters to the editor
and the personal ads that most readers tend to skip.*

*'Indeed,' our guest replied, 'I work in the Lyceum
as manager for Henry Irving's theatrical productions,
including all domestic and foreign tours. That is perhaps also one of the problems in my marriage, that
in recent years I have not been able to give sufficient
attention to the well-being of my wife and the daily
goings-on in my home.'*

'You were married in Ireland, I understand. When was that?'

'Yes, I'm afraid my accent testifies to my Irish heritage,' replied Stoker, who was beginning to adjust somewhat to Holmes's pertinent method of asking questions. 'My wife's name is Florence, Florence Balcombe, and our marriage took place on the 4th of December, 1878 in Dublin. Soon after we moved to London, a year later, our only son was born. In addition to my daily work, I have always been a writer: dramatic reviews, articles, stories and novels, on which I spend many of my free hours.'

'And what exactly is the present problem with your wife?' Holmes wanted to know. I sensed an ever so slight impatience in his voice.

'Yes...,' Stoker began with a sigh. His large body seemed to get in his way, as if he could not express himself freely under the weight of it. 'I... found out that my wife goes out without telling me anything about it and then stays away for long hours. I would like to know where she is going and what she is doing there. I am afraid there is something she is hiding from me, something that might get me or herself or both of us in trouble.' In making these assumptions, Mr Stoker looked at us in turn, with a painful expression on his face.

'What are you thinking of?' asked Holmes, slowly closing his eyes and taking a deep puff of his pipe, the smoke of which he held in his mouth for some time, before letting it cloud out again. 'A relationship? An addiction? A whim?' The expression on Stoker's face *now became even more laborious than before. He clearly did not dare to make any concrete speculations about his domestic problem. 'Why don't you just ask her?' suggested Holmes.*

'To be perfectly honest, Sir, that I do not dare, because my wife blames me for my frequent and sometimes prolonged absence from home. With Henry Irving I am regularly on tour for weeks or months on end in England or Ireland or Scotland and occasionally even for a longer period of time to America and Canada. I hardly feel in a position to ask her to account for her absence from our home during a few hours. Moreover, many of the attempts I make towards having a proper conversation between us come to nothing. But as her husband, I am worried and I do feel that I have a right to know what is going on. Yesterday, someone told me, that after I had left the house to go to the theatre, she left on foot and did not come home until late in the afternoon.'

'My dear Mr Stoker,' Holmes responded, now with a distinctly impatient tone, 'I don't have much experience with life in a marital state myself. But should not a married woman be able to just go out during the day, without her husband immediately attaching the wildest speculations to her behaviour?'

Stoker looked around with a tormented expression. He was visibly struggling to say what was on his mind, and the pronouncement that finally followed was spoken in a pinched voice, looking at neither of us: 'But my wife was dressed as a man.'

After this sudden confession our visitor was silent, and he took turns looking at us with a rigid gaze. I immediately saw that the case was now beginning to interest Sherlock Holmes. Until then he had sat somewhat listlessly, seemingly more engrossed in the taste of his tobacco than in the conversation, but upon hearing this detail, the expression in his eyes lighted up, and I knew from experience that the little wheels of his brain had begun to turn.

'The person who told you this was sure of that?' he asked.

'Absolutely, there can be no mistake. The reliability of my spokesman is beyond doubt.'

'And what would you like us to do for you?' asked Holmes, putting his gently smouldering clay pipe to the side.

'I would like to know what my wife is doing in the city in this disguise, so that, if necessary, I can perhaps avert any dangers to our marriage, to her and to myself and to our son. Here in London, we are in the middle of a series of performances of King Arthur, and this afternoon I have to go to Birmingham, Leeds and Liverpool for a few days to prepare for a new tour, but on my return, I hope I may expect to hear some explanation from you for this strange behaviour of my wife.'

Holmes promised that he would get to work immediately, wrote down some practical details and a little later we said goodbye to Mr Stoker, promising that he would hear from us in a few days.

'Your friend is forgetting his hat,' Holmes said teasingly to our visitor as he hurried out of the room. With an awkward movement Mr Stoker reached back to grab his headgear and left.

'Well, my dear Watson, what do you make of it?' exclaimed Holmes, after the door had closed behind the troubled husband.

'I absolutely have no idea,' I replied, "but the man is clearly nerve-ridden. It looks as if the merits of marriage as a form of life can vary considerably from person to person."

'And it also looks as if tomorrow morning we are going to do a little dressing-up ourselves, to find out where Mrs Stoker likes to spend her days,' Holmes replied.

I will not bore the reader with a detailed reconstruction of how Sherlock Holmes and I followed Mrs Stoker's movements at an appropriate distance for three consecutive days. She preferred to cover long distances in the city on foot, perhaps from a personal predilection or in the hope that her movements would thus be less easy to trace.

Sherlock Holmes is very adept at disguises, and on each of the three days he had a totally different appearance, so far removed from his accustomed personality that on each day it was only with some effort that I recognised him at our agreed meeting place close to the Stokers' home. The first day he was a delivery man, with a cap and a shoulder bag and some not too heavy packages, the second day an office clerk, and the third an ordinary seaman with a small duffel bag. I myself did not make too much effort to dress up, but I did choose a different colour jacket and a different head covering for each of the three days.

The first day Mrs Stoker came out of her house in a long raincoat with a hat and a walking stick. From *a distance I could not make out her face sharply, but I had the impression she had made up herself somewhat, and I must say that as a young man she looked rather plausible. It is amazing how a headgear alone can determine the image of someone's person, although being in the know I could imagine that behind this disguise was a not unattractive woman of about thirty-five years of age. Holmes and I, standing on opposite pavements, gave each other a subtle signal, and off we went.*

Our very civilised pursuit began in a north-eastern direction, via Victoria Station, over the Victoria Road to Westminster Bridge, then a stretch along the river to The Temple, where she turned left. At that moment, Holmes, raising his hand to his cap, signalled that he knew enough for the day and that we could go back home. It had been a long walk, nearly a full hour.

The second day, Mrs Stoker surprised us by suddenly no longer appearing in male disguise, but simply as the neat and indeed rather attractive lady that she really is. That day she went for a much shorter walk northward via Smith Street, left onto King's Road and then right via Markham Street to Elystan Street towards the Fulham Road. Halfway up Brompton Road, Holmes had had enough, and in silence we took a carriage back to Baker Street. On the third day, after no more ten minutes, Holmes called off our chase, as soon as he realised that she would take the same route as on day two.

Several times during these walks I had the feeling that we had embarked on a nonsensical expedition, but on the evening of the second day Holmes intimated that the peregrinations of Mrs Stoker were clear enough to him. Experience has taught me that at such an early stage of Holmes's investigations it is better not to bother him with questions, so we sat silently for a while. From the way Holmes was smoking his clay pipe and sitting with his eyes closed, I deduced that he was still working on some loose ends in the story.

In the afternoon of the third day, after Holmes had exchanged his appearance as a shabby seaman for his familiar dressing gown, he played the violin for some time, to take his thoughts from the everyday misery in which his clients tend to immerse him, while I read a number of recent newspapers, such as I found in piles on the floor around Holmes's chair.

Earlier than I expected, Holmes announced that it was time to invite Mr Stoker for a brief discussion of our findings, assuming that he had meanwhile returned from his travels. That turned out to be the case, and an invitation by telegram brought him to Baker Street less than two hours later.

On his second visit, our client, if possible, seemed even more tense than during our first meeting. He did not even have time to answer a polite question about his activities in the North. Apparently, he was eager to hear our report.

'I believe,' said Sherlock Holmes to our guest, who had sat down in the same place as before, 'that you need not be so worried. In the past few days your wife has undertaken things that are completely on the right side of the law and of the human mind.'

'I hope you will let me be the judge of that myself,' Stoker countered, somewhat piqued. 'Please just tell me where she has been.'

'Alright, if it is just the facts that you want,' Holmes responded measuredly, 'then I will tell you. We have traced your wife's movements for three days: first, she was present dressed as a man at The Old Bailey on the final day of the libel trial of Oscar Wilde against the Marquess of Queensberry. The other two days in her own female attire she had an appointment with the Provost of the London Oratory at Old Brompton Road.'

At that moment, something baffling occurred. These simple statements produced an acute crisis in our visitor. He began to breathe heavily, his shoulders jerking up and down, his face flushing red and then becoming quite pale, and he stood up with a haggard expression, looking for... yes, for what? Before we could do anything, I saw his eyes turn away and his large body fell back into the chair, with such a dull thud that the retorts, burettes and Erlenmeyer flasks in the display case behind him rang dangerously.

'Quick, Watson, give him air,' Holmes called out, leaping up. I immediately loosened Stoker's collar, while Holmes fetched a glass of water, to which he added a sip of brandy. It seemed like an eternity until the man returned to his senses and it took a few minutes before he was able to keep his eyes open a little longer and drink a few gulps, so that his consciousness gradually returned, together with his normal complexion.

'I am very sorry that I have upset you so much,' said Holmes, 'But you were so insistent on the facts that I gave them to you in all simplicity.'

'Are you alright now?' I enquired, checking his pulse.

Stoker could only respond in mumbled words: 'Terrible,' 'What a disaster,' 'I knew this was going to happen,' and more of such muddled complaints.

As soon as Stoker had fully come back to himself, he wanted to know if Sherlock Holmes was completely sure of his case. 'Absolutely,' Holmes replied. 'Apart from our own observations, on both locations there was someone on my behalf who followed her into both premises and observed her there for some time. But perhaps,' he added, 'you would be kind enough to tell us why these two addresses are so terrifying. Oscar Wilde's failed libel trial has completely dominated the newspapers these past few days,' said Holmes, pointing to the piles to the left and right of his armchair, 'and this court case has undoubtedly revealed strange and unpleasant things, but where in your eyes lies the disaster?'

'The writer you are referring to,' Stoker began, after a prolonged silence, 'I prefer not to mention his name—competed for my wife's hand for a few years in the past, and he still exerts a strong influence over her that I find unhealthy and undesirable. Moreover, through his spiritual powers he has for some time been drawing her towards the Roman Catholic Church. I fear that she will convert to Catholicism because of these disastrous forces.'

'That is a whole new dimension to the story,' Sherlock Holmes responded. 'I had inferred from your wife's conduct that she is personally interested in the Wilde-case. Since in the Courtroom of The Old Bailey no women were allowed to enter, I understood that disguising herself as a man was the only way for her to gain access there. That there was a connection with an appointment she had in the Oratory is now clear to me, but since that earlier love story was not known to me, I could not possibly have taken that into account.' After some hesitation, Holmes added, 'What else could Dr Watson and I do for you?'

'Well,' Mr Stoker mused doubtfully, 'I wouldn't know that, but I will think about it. I am very unhappy with the whole situation. In any case, you will serve my interests best if I can count on your complete discretion, because the whole thing is quite worrisome to me.'

Holmes and I made that commitment, of course, and said goodbye to our client, who closed the door behind him, lost in thought. The following morning, all the newspapers reported that after his lost libel trial Oscar Wilde had been arrested in the Cadogan Hotel and that he would be prosecuted on the basis of Section 11 of the Criminal Law Amendment Act.

Over the next few days, I was not in touch with Holmes. Mary had meanwhile returned home, and the somewhat chilly spring weather of the previous weeks produced a regular stream of patients in my practice, with the kind of complaints that in 99% of cases tend to pass by themselves. The task of a doctor is no *more, but also no less, to single out that one percent to which a meaningful or even necessary treatment can be applied.*

When I came to Baker Street again about two weeks later at Holmes's initiative to catch up on life, I found him in the grip of two new cases for which he had been called in. Although he told me about them with some eagerness, it turned out that he had mainly asked me to come over since he was still mulling over the case of Mr and Mrs Stoker. The newspapers had been filled with growing excitement about Oscar Wilde's upcoming criminal trial, which was to begin on the 26th, again at The Old Bailey. Holmes and I agreed that the immorality of which the well-known playwright was accused was not at all a matter for the law, but rather for medical science and its modern ramifications. The whole story had continued to occupy my mind over the past two weeks, partly because of the impending doom for an extremely talented and astute author, and partly because Holmes and I had seen with our own eyes how much this tragedy had taken hold of the life and marital happiness of the Stoker couple.

By now spring had arrived, and Holmes was sitting in his chair smoking with the curtains half-closed against the bright sunlight. Just I was wondering whether there had been a reason behind Holmes's invitation to come round, he handed me The Pall Mall Gazette, *in which he had encircled the following announcement:*

SALE of OSCAR WILDE'S EFFECTS

Messrs. Bullock, of High Holborn, will tomorrow sell
the effects of Oscar Wilde at 16, Tite Street. The sale
includes many valuable prints, among others some of
the prized Arundel Society's re-productions. Carlyle's
writing table and Wilde's well-known collection of
Moorish pottery and old blue and white china are
expected to cause much keen competition.

*'If you feel like it,' Holmes said, 'we can stop by there
to have a look. There will no doubt be a viewing today.'*
*When we drove past the Botanic Gardens of the
Chelsea Hospital into the lower end of Tite Street about
an hour later, it was immediately clear that something
was going on at No. 16. From a distance, it seemed
more like a disturbance than a viewing for an auction.
An enforced sale ordered by creditors rarely produces
an uplifting spectacle, Holmes observed, as we got
out of our carriage and walked towards the crowd of
people jostling to get into the house in order to view
the goods on sale. There was a lot of pushing and pull-
ing and the rudeness of the prospective buyers and
especially of the traders was in stark contrast to the
obvious sophistication with which the house was decorated and furnished.*
*With a copy of the simple auction catalogue in
hand, Holmes and I squeezed ourselves through the
crowded corridors and disorderly rooms of the house.
Drawers had been pulled out of cabinets, so that their
contents lay in a mess on the floor. With a gesture*

and a raised eyebrow Holmes pointed out to me that
in some cases the locks had been forced. The largest
part of the lots in the catalogue was dedicated to
books and paintings.

'Look here, Watson,' Holmes said to me suddenly
with a straight face. We were standing in the corridor
on the first floor of the house, where it was a hustle
and bustle, just as downstairs. The tone of his voice,
as muffled as it was commanding, indicated complete
seriousness on the part of my friend. I immediately did
as he asked and together we pretended for a while to
be studying a picture hanging on the wall, showing a
group of merrymakers dancing at the edge of a forest.

'Let us go,' Holmes suggested not more than a
minute later. He had made a note of something in
the auction catalogue. I followed him, still surprised
by his sudden change of behaviour, as we squeezed
our way downstairs to the front door. In our carriage
back to Baker Street, Holmes was silent, and once
home he sent two telegrams, one of them to Mr Stoker,
asking him to come by at 5 o'clock in the afternoon
the next day.

'I'm sorry, Watson,' Holmes said, 'but I'm afraid
there is not much else we can do today. Perhaps
tomorrow will offer new possibilities,' he added with
an enigmatic smile. Then we talked for some time
about the two other cases that occupied him at the
time, 'The Drowned Architect' and 'The Kidnapped Italian Duchess'.

The next afternoon we were ready for the third
visit from Mr Stoker, who entered our sitting room

punctually at 5 o'clock and after a brief mutual greeting took his by now familiar seat across from us. He had been surprised, he said, by the invitation to come over, as he had not expected Sherlock Holmes to be still working on his case.

'Mr Stoker,' Holmes addressed him somewhat sternly, 'you had previously promised to provide us with all the facts and circumstances that might be relevant for our endeavour to help you, but I regret to say that there is one more thing that I would have liked to hear about from you, and which I now have had to find out for myself, in an attempt to resolve satisfactorily the matter you put into our hands.'

Stoker watched Holmes anxiously, clearly not knowing what to expect. Then out of the left pocket of his dressing gown Holmes pulled a small gold crucifix on a slender chain, which he dangled back and forth from his left hand between the three of us.

It may be too much to say that Stoker recoiled from this little piece of jewellery, but he looked at it fixedly and with wide eyes of bewilderment, as if it were not a Christian but a diabolical symbol which posed a great threat to him.

'How... Where on earth did you get that from?' he stammered.

'That was very simple,' Holmes said airily, 'I had it purchased earlier today by my brother Mycroft in an auction sale at an address in Tite Street, Chelsea. It came in a tin box as part of lot No. 237, described in the catalogue as 'A very large quantity of toys.' I paid six shillings for the whole box. You may want to take *a closer look at this little pendant. There is something engraved on it.'*

'Unbelievable. I knew this existed,' Stoker began slowly, more to himself than to us, but he did not move his head an inch closer to the crucifix. 'My wife showed me this once, before our marriage, almost twenty years ago now. But I didn't know its present whereabouts. That you tracked this down...' All the while, Stoker did not reach out for the crucifix, but let it hang in the empty air between us.

'Yesterday I went with my friend Dr Watson to the viewing day of this public sale,' Holmes began, meanwhile letting the small jewel drop onto the side-table next to Stoker's chair. 'Almost immediately I recognised your wife, whose footsteps we followed a few weeks ago at your request. She wore a hat and veil, and she was the only woman present, which attracted my attention in the first place. I saw that she was doing something with this box of children's toys, which was on view among so many other objects, but I couldn't quite make out whether she was putting something in or taking something out or if she was just lifting the box to have a better look at it. And now, my dear Mr Stoker,' Sherlock Holmes added with a sugary smile, 'apart from this little golden crucifix that I would like to give you as a present, I am now the proud owner of a considerable number of pewter soldiers and toy trains.'

Mr. Stoker thanked him profusely and some moments later stepped out the door with the crucifix in his pocket, the little pendant having been folded by

Holmes into a torn-off piece of newspaper. All the time, Stoker had not touched the metal of the cross by hand even once.

Holmes sent one of his Baker Street boys after our visitor to see what he would do with the crucifix. Less than an hour later the boy reported that Stoker had gone straight to a jeweller to have the gold melted down and turn into a smooth ring with a solitary garnet. What he subsequently did with the ring, is a matter that concerns only himself, but at least the riddle of 'The Golden Crucifix' had been solved by Sherlock Holmes, even without Mr Stoker having expressly asked him to. In that respect, this case is unique, among the many dozens of adventures I have experienced with my friend, ever since A Study in Scarlet.

16

MISSING

In our time, Oscar Wilde's reputation as a writer and as a cultural personality is virtually undisputed, but at the time of his death on the 30th of November, 1900, his social disgrace was complete. As a former prisoner, as a homosexual, as a criminal, as an exile who had left England never to return, he was an outcast, someone who could hardly count on any respect or a minimum of appreciation for his person or his literary work outside a circle of close friends. Even in Normandy, to which he had first fled after his release from prison, and later in Paris and elsewhere, English tourists were almost without exception disgusted by his mere presence.

Throughout his life, many of Wilde's friends, acquaintances and fellow writers have recorded their memories of him. Inevitably, these versions do not always agree with each other. In fact, you wish those descriptions, laid out in biographies, memoirs, interviews, and letters, would provide much more detail. The ultimate intangibility of detail is what is most exasperating about the past, the fact that minor questions have become insoluble, that a close-up image is impossible. Perhaps when you peek around the corner of the

*Is this perhaps Oscar Wilde in June of 1900, walking with
a younger friend, both in white summer suits, over the
grounds of the 'Exposition Universelle' in Paris, with the
Italian Pavilion in the background? If so, it would be the
last photograph taken of the writer while he was alive.*

imagination, you can observe something of focused historical
truth. That is what I have tried to do in this book, if only to
find the answer to a small, but persistent question.

So, has the search for Florence Balcombe's little golden
cross yielded us anything? Not the jewel itself, unfortunately,
at least not in its original material form. But we have visited
Oscar Wilde up close in Dublin, at the home of his girlfriend,
and we have followed his trail to Greece. We have seen how

his years as a student in Oxford, followed by his formative tour in America, laid the foundation for his further development as a man of letters and above all as an artist of life. And we have watched over his deathbed in Paris, together with Reggie Turner.

'Not the fruit of the experience, but the experience itself is the goal.' That wisdom from Walter Pater, one of Oscar Wilde's heroes as a student, remained the writer's lifelong motto. It was a piece of wisdom that took him, like it did Dorian Gray, to new places, exciting company, and adventurous circumstances, where he hoped to gain new experiences. Some of these experiences went far beyond those of his bourgeois contemporaries, but then they also reached ever further than Wilde's own previous boundaries. A combination of what the ancient Greeks called ὕβρις (hubris), reckless over-confidence towards the fate of the gods, and an almost masochistic fatalism, meant that with his increasingly extreme behaviour he could not and would not prevent his tragic fall. His reception *in extremis* into the arms of the Roman Catholic Church, after several years of pain and suffering, was a conciliatory conclusion to a martyrdom, which the writer himself has transformed into a kind of self-gospel in *De Profundis*.

Indeed, Wilde's life can be read and reread as a gospel. The parallelism of his martyrdom with the ill-fated life and crucifixion of Jesus Christ was identified as such by himself in the long letter which he wrote from Reading Prison to his beloved Alfred Douglas. In it, he even presents Christ as a symbolic figure for the life and suffering of all artists and poets. You don't have to go to Oscar Wilde for understatement; his favourite field is exaggeration, satire, and paradox. And they abound in his plays, in his essays, in his short stories and in the epigrams handed down from him. Especially in the flashy paradox he is such a master, that the fireworks of his aphorisms, epigrams, enchanting fairy tales and pointed characterisations often succeed in hiding his shortcomings from view.

These shortcomings should not be denied. Wilde's use of language is often very poetic, but he was not really a great poet. His long poem *The Sphinx* (1894), for example, in which a young man tries to find out the sexual secrets of a sphinx and finally resorts to—yes—a crucifix, is almost bursting at the seams with sought-after and exquisite rhyming words. It is decorative and exotic, and it is very ingeniously put together. Yet it is questionable whether it is really impressive as a poetic text. In his first and only collection of poems, simply entitled *Poems* (1881), the poet sometimes leans heavily on the work of illustrious predecessors and older contemporaries. Furthermore, behind Wilde's dandyistic aestheticism and his advocacy of women's fashion, interior art and art for art's sake, a colossal narcissistic conceit was invariably eager to show itself. And in contrast to his reputation as a champion of gay emancipation, in our time there are accusations of paedophilia and grooming of underage boys. While one observer may sympathise from the present with Wilde as an LGBTIQ+ personality locked in a conventional marriage, another might look with contempt on the unscrupulousness of his self-indulgence.

Enough criticism. I have tried in this book not to exaggerate my admiration for Oscar Wilde but let the same apply to the criticism. Incidentally, Wilde himself had nothing against exaggeration; in fact, he was a true proponent of it. As he wrote in a review of a collection of essays by Walter Pater, whom he greatly admired: 'Where there is no exaggeration there is no love, and where there is no love there is no understanding.'

The 'two sweet years' of being in love, albeit often from a distance, with Florence Balcombe must have seemed to Wilde in later life a kind of child's play: having tea at her parents' home, going to church with her on Christmas Day, giving her a little golden crucifix with their names or initials engraved in it. One can hardly imagine more innocent pastimes. On the other hand, at some point he must have realised that these too were experiences; not the fruit of experience, but the experience itself, and therefore a perfectly legitimate and formative episode. It is clear on and between the lines of his later letters to various people how fondly he remembered that time with his Florrie.

If this fondness was reciprocated even in the slightest measure by Florence, then it is quite understandable that Bram Stoker was very tense about the role that Oscar Wilde played so close to his marital and professional life. Stoker's radical harshness in keeping Oscar Wilde's name out of all his writings and correspondence speaks volumes and seems to have driven Wilde's ghost into his subconscious, from which he drew to a considerable degree for the figure of his lurid Count Dracula.

Both Oscar Wilde and Bram Stoker looked with envy upon the easy physicality, sexuality, and boundless love, embodied by their distant hero Walt Whitman. So much looseness, so much freedom, such unboundedness and at the same time such power of expression and such unbridled poetry. During America's Gilded Age it was hard enough for Whitman to maintain his way of life. In Victorian England it was completely out of the question.

Each in their own way, Wilde and Stoker were condemned to an imprisoned existence during their lifetime. In the biographical literature about her two lovers the beautiful, talented Florence Balcombe, despite her strength and her talents, has been reduced to an almost invisible connection between these two complex men. It was not until January 2020 that she, along with a number of other historical personalities, was added as a 'missing person' to the *Dictionary of Irish Biography*. At last, belatedly and only in print, she was reunited with her admirer Oscar Wilde and her troubled but hard-working husband Bram Stoker. And rightly so, for as the hidden link between these protagonists from Victorian literary history, Florence Balcombe deserves to be visible in her own right, just as shiny as the little golden crucifix that I have been looking for and that unfortunately I will never hold in my hand.

NOTE

I t is virtually impossible to acknowledge all the historical data and references in this book. In some instances I have mentioned an important source in the text, but the inclusion, in a bibliography or in footnotes, of all the biographies, editions of correspondence, magazine articles, memoirs, travel guides, monographs, maps, websites, auction catalogues and newspaper archives that I have used, would have given this book an undesirable heaviness. An additional advantage of not accounting for all these sources lies in the open spaces in historical and biographical reality, and the possibilities of literary fantasy. Most of the fabrications presented here—clearly distinguished by being printed in italic—are in theory perfectly possible, and my basic idea was that a small riddle from the past, such as a vanished jewel, can be studied fruitfully with a biographer's eye, but can perhaps only be solved with a little help of the imagination.

MA

ABOUT THE
AUTHOR

M aarten Asscher (°1957) studied law and Assyriology
at Leiden University in the Netherlands. He started
his career in literary publishing in 1980 and became the
Dutch publisher of writers such as Carlos Fuentes, Primo
Levi, Amos Oz, James Salter and Wisława Szymborska. In
2004, after six years as a cultural policy advisor at the Dutch
Ministry of Education, Culture and Science, he went on to
become director and co-owner of the Athenaeum Bookshop
in Amsterdam. In 2018 he decided to devote his energy full-
time to writing and to translating poetry.

From 1992 onwards he published novels, short stories and novellas, and several books of essays. In 2015 he obtained a PhD in comparative literature with a dissertation on imprisonment as a literary experience. Most of his books have also appeared in German translation. He has translated poetry by Paul Valéry, Albrecht Haushofer and Fernando Pessoa and produced a Dutch translation of Oscar Wilde's *The Ballad of Reading Gaol.*

The members of the British Oscar Wilde Society awarded Asscher the first prize in their 2024 Wilde Wit Competition for his Wildean epigram: "In art, originality is too quickly applauded, in life it is usually punished."

In 2015 Four Winds Press published his essay collection *Apples and Oranges: In Praise of Comparisons,* translated by Brian Doyle Du-Breuil. *Oscar Wilde's Crucifix: A Biographical Experiment* is the author's first book written in English.

Maarten Asscher is married and lives in Amsterdam. He has three adult daughters.